D0088615

More Praise for *Crunch Time*

"In your high-pressure moments, don't just try to survive. Apply Rick and Judd's coaching and you will thrive!"

—**Marshall Goldsmith, Thinkers50 #1 Leadership Thinker in the World and bestselling author**

"In business as in baseball, your ability to perform under pressure can make or break your career. *Crunch Time* will teach you how to thrive in high-stakes situations."

—**Travis Bradberry, bestselling coauthor of *Emotional Intelligence 2.0***

"Every day is Crunch Time in New York. When I was the New York Mets' manager, Rick was the perfect fit to be my pitching coach. He has a unique ability to reframe pressure situations to maximize performance. *Crunch Time* is a must-read to optimize your performance in your own 'Big Apple.'"

—**Willie Randolph, former Manager, New York Mets, six-time All-Star, and six-time World Series Champion**

"Rick Peterson is a national treasure. His storytelling is matched only by his hard-earned wisdom, and I'm thrilled he's teamed with Judd Hoekstra to bring you the best of both. Their book is packed with insights on being at your best when the pressure is highest."

—**Cade Massey, PhD, Professor, The Wharton School**

"At one time or another, at work or at home, all of us have felt like the whole game was riding on our shoulders. Rick and Judd apply what Rick has learned working with elite athletes to not only lift that burden but enable you to perform at your best."

—**Susan Torroella, Executive Vice President, Wellness Corporate Solutions, and *Fortune Small Business* Best Boss Award recipient**

"Your heart is racing, your stomach is churning, and all eyes are upon you; your next move will decide whether you win or lose. Sales professionals, like professional athletes, know this scenario all too well. *Crunch Time* is a fun read that helps you take advantage of your adrenaline and make the most of high-pressure situations."

—**Bill Mathews, Associate Vice President, Facilities Growth, Aramark**

"Rick Peterson has always applied a distinctive blend of insight and creativity in his out-of-the-box approach to solving problems. With *Crunch Time*, he and Judd Hoekstra lay out, in a compelling and entertaining way, an approach to dealing with pressure that can help all of us in our tough personal and professional moments."

—**Bill Squadron, Professor, Columbia University, and former President, Bloomberg Sports**

"*Crunch Time* has already helped me reframe one issue, allowing us to save six figures. This is an amazingly inspirational book with examples everyone can relate to. I've shared this new knowledge with our team, resulting in a renewed alignment, confidence, and success!"
—**Yogesh Madhvani, CEO, SimplexDiam, Inc.**

"I've had the privilege of interviewing hundreds of professional athletes and coaches, and few are as insightful as Rick Peterson. He has a gift for distilling complex concepts into understandable terms. He is famous for developing the best pitchers in the world, of course, but he can teach us all about performing under pressure. The only thing better than a Rick Peterson interview is a Rick Peterson book."
—**Lee Jenkins, Lead Writer, *Sports Illustrated***

"I wish I'd read this book sooner! I had an experience where I choked hard core. The more I tried to figure out why I was striking out, the greater the pressure became. I could no longer think clearly. Reading *Crunch Time*, with its practical techniques and relatable examples, I can now see what I will do differently next time."
—**Laurie Cooke, CEO, Healthcare Businesswomen's Association**

"Nobody knows more than Rick Peterson about dealing with pressure, whether it be the seventh game of the World Series or a real-world situation."
—**Jerry Reinsdorf, Chairman and owner, Chicago White Sox and Chicago Bulls**

"Fascinating behind-the-scenes stories about how elite leaders, coaches, and performers have learned to thrive under pressure. The best part is that the lessons apply to all of us in our everyday pressure situations."
—**Jon Gordon, bestselling author of *Training Camp* and *The Energy Bus***

"Rick has years of experience teaching professional and amateur pitchers how to maximize their true potential, how to embrace pressure and avoid crumbling under the weight of others' expectations. He and Judd now team up to share those experiences in *Crunch Time*, a must-read for anyone looking to conquer pressure in the business world or in daily life!"
—**Jim Duquette, former General Manager, New York Mets and Baltimore Orioles, and Major League Baseball analyst**

"I love Rick's progressive and out-of-the-box thinking. He helped me improve as a major league pitcher at the back end of my career in the pressure cooker of New York with the Mets. In *Crunch Time*, Rick and Judd provide a GPS for you to perform your best under pressure."
—**Al Leiter, nineteen-year major league pitcher, two-time World Series Champion, two-time All-Star, and Emmy award–winning Major League Baseball analyst**

"Rick has the deepest knowledge of pitching that I have come across in my career. He helped me immensely. This includes sharing wisdom in areas beyond baseball, such as dealing with pressure. I encourage you to dig deep into *Crunch Time*. The lessons last a lifetime."
—**Barry Zito, fifteen-year major league pitcher, World Series Champion, three-time All-Star, and Cy Young Award winner**

"*Crunch Time* succinctly defined and taught me concepts and techniques that are relevant across business, personal, and athletic challenges. So easy to grasp and apply, and with enough variety for just about any situation. Thanks for helping me find ways to 'change the station,' remember that it's okay to relax under pressure, and simply perform better."
—**Tracey Roberts, Chief Human Resource Officer, Weber-Stephen Products LLC, busy mom, and "weekend warrior" triathlete**

"On the surface, *Crunch Time* seems to skillfully address a specific life situation—the physiological and psychological response to pressure. Upon reflection, its application is much more than that. From public speaking to parenting to corporate leadership, the richness of the life lessons that are incorporated in this engaging and relatable text is, in fact, enormously broad. So, sit back, relax, and reframe your perspective."
—**James G. Conroy, President and CEO, Boot Barn**

"Contrary to what many of us assume, it is not our body or possessions that determine happiness and success; it is the state of our mind. This book will help you go from stress and fear to optimal performance when it matters most, by teaching you how to train your mind."
—**Dr. Rogier Hoenders, psychiatrist and Director, Center for Integrative Psychiatry, Lentis, the Netherlands**

"*Crunch Time* brings the magic of the Professor (as Rick was known throughout the big leagues) to the reader in an engaging, inspiring way. Judd translates Rick's success as a pitching coach into the everyday pressures we face at work, at school, at home, and in the community. The proven power of reframing—under the most trying of circumstances—can help shift our heads, hearts, and hands from victim to victor. You need *Crunch Time* to be your best!"
—**S. Chris Edmonds, author of the Amazon bestseller *The Culture Engine***

"It is our mindset that distinguishes those who truly perform under pressure and not just our skill level. *Crunch Time* taught me how to coach my team to come up with new ways to rethink a situation and see it as a new opportunity and that they have what it takes to succeed! There is a lot to learn from Rick's coaching with elite athletes, and it definitely translates to the business world."
—**Charlene Prounis, CEO, Flashpoint Medica**

"Time and again we hear anecdotes about how sports results can relate to business decisions. Rick Peterson, who has always thought beyond the diamond, has coauthored an essential read to help you succeed in business, sports, and life."

—Joe Favorito, veteran sports entertainment marketing executive and Professor, Columbia University

"As someone who challenges convention and explores new ideas, Rick Peterson is an important voice not only in baseball but also in finding your personal best."

—Tom Verducci, bestselling coauthor of *The Yankee Years* and Emmy Award–winning Major League Baseball analyst

"Using engaging stories from high-pressure situations in business, sports, and life, Rick Peterson and Judd Hoekstra give you the mental tools you need to deliver when tension is high and everyone is depending on you. A key part of leadership is learning; using that learning to develop an engaged and passionate culture is vital."

—Garry Ridge, President and CEO, WD-40 Company

"This is one of those books I'll keep close to me, to pull out when I need encouragement and coaching. I wouldn't be surprised to find myself reviewing it again and again."

—Martha Lawrence, coauthor of *Trust Works!*

"*Crunch Time* is an instant classic. Rick's unique wisdom on the baseball diamond and Judd's ability to translate that wisdom across numerous work, sports, and life situations has produced the definitive prescription for clutch performance. This book has already improved my professional mindset and my golf game!"

—Douglas Madenberg, Principal, Retail Feedback Group, and coauthor of *Feedback Rules!*

"*Crunch Time* entertains while providing concrete, actionable, personal behavior-changing advice. Great stories, great advice . . . a great read."

—Mark Censoprano, Chief Marketing Officer, Aspen Dental Management

CRUNCH TIME

HOW TO BE YOUR **BEST** WHEN IT MATTERS **MOST**

CRUNCH TIME

HOW TO BE YOUR **BEST** WHEN IT MATTERS **MOST**

Rick Peterson
Director of Pitching Development for the Baltimore Orioles and Pitching Coach for the Oakland Athletics during the Moneyball Era

Judd Hoekstra
Coauthor of the bestselling Leading at a Higher Level *and* Who Killed Change? *and Vice President, The Ken Blanchard Companies*

Foreword by Billy Beane
Executive Vice President of Baseball Operations, Oakland Athletics

Berrett–Koehler Publishers, Inc.
a BK Business book

Berrett-Koehler Publishers, Inc.
1333 Broadway, Suite 1000
Oakland, CA 94612-1921
Tel: (510) 817-2277   Fax: (510) 817-2278
www.bkconnection.com

Ordering Information

Quantity sales. Special discounts are available on quantity purchases by corporations, associations, and others. For details, contact the "Special Sales Department" at the Berrett-Koehler address above.

Individual sales. Berrett-Koehler publications are available through most bookstores. They can also be ordered directly from Berrett-Koehler: Tel: (800) 929-2929; Fax: (802) 864-7626; www.bkconnection.com.

Orders for college textbook/course adoption use. Please contact Berrett-Koehler: Tel: (800) 929-2929; Fax: (802) 864-7626.

Orders by U.S. trade bookstores and wholesalers. Please contact Ingram Publisher Services, Tel: (800) 509-4887; Fax: (800) 838-1149; E-mail: customer.service@ingrampublisherservices.com; or visit www.ingrampublisherservices.com/Ordering for details about electronic ordering.

Berrett-Koehler and the BK logo are registered trademarks of Berrett-Koehler Publishers, Inc.

Printed in the United States of America

Berrett-Koehler books are printed on long-lasting acid-free paper. When it is available, we choose paper that has been manufactured by environmentally responsible processes. These may include using trees grown in sustainable forests, incorporating recycled paper, minimizing chlorine in bleaching, or recycling the energy produced at the paper mill.

Library of Congress Cataloging-in-Publication Data

Names: Peterson, Rick, 1954– author. | Hoekstra, Judd, 1970– author.
Title: Crunch time : how to be your best when it matters most / Rick Peterson
  and Judd Hoekstra.
Description: First Edition. | Oakland, CA : Berrett-Koehler Publishers,
  [2016] | Includes bibliographical references and index.
Identifiers: LCCN 2016034050 | ISBN 9781626567696 (pbk.)
Subjects: LCSH: Stress (Psychology) | Self-confidence. | Self-control.
Classification: LCC BF575.S75 P468 2016 | DDC 155.9/042—dc23
LC record available at https://lccn.loc.gov/2016034050

First Edition
21 20 19 18 17   16 10 9 8 7 6 5 4 3 2 1

Interior design and production by Happenstance Type-O-Rama

To my wife, Lelia O'Connor
You are my beacon of light and inspiration to
illuminate my life in 108 ways.

—Rick Peterson

To Sherry, Julia, and Cole
May you seek and find the opportunities
in every challenge.

—Judd Hoekstra

Table of Contents

Preface

The privilege of a lifetime is to be the best of who you
are and to exercise that privilege every day.

—*RICK PETERSON*

In the spring of 2013, I received a call from someone seeking
to write a book with leadership guru Dr. Ken Blanchard. After
working with Ken for almost 15 years, I've heard this request many
times. However, this request was unlike any of the others. I stood
up and took notice.

The caller was Rick Peterson, the most renowned pitching coach
on the planet. He coached the Oakland Athletics pitching staff
during the famed *Moneyball* era. He also coached a New York Mets
pitching staff comprised of All-Stars, Cy Young Award winners,
and Hall of Famers. Being a former college baseball player and life-
long fan of the game, I was thrilled to be speaking with Rick. When
it comes to pitching coaches, he is *the* pitching coach.

Rick shared that he felt a kinship with Ken, the coauthor of the
runaway bestseller *The One Minute Manager*. He highlighted how a
pitching coach is the ultimate One Minute Manager. He is responsible for setting clear goals, praising progress toward the goals, and
redirecting performance when it's off track. But Rick also pointed
out one big difference.

A pitching coach doesn't operate in your typical office environment. He is the only coach in professional sports who provides

in-game coaching on the field of play. He must calm his pitcher down in front of millions of fans, with the game on the line, in 30 seconds or less. Also, everyone watching will know within minutes whether or not the coaching worked.

Ken let Rick know he would love to work with him but was committed to other book projects for the next few years. Knowing my expertise and passion for leadership, coaching, and sports, Ken recommended I work with Rick. When I suggested this idea to Rick, he welcomed me with open arms. So began our odyssey.

In addition to my excitement to share Rick's unique perspective and expertise with you, I had a secret and selfish reason for working with him. Despite my success in amateur athletics and now in business, I have vivid nightmares from choking at crunch time. I'm not alone. Performing at less than your best in high-pressure situations is a universal problem. I see it wherever I turn—at work and in everyday life.

Help is on the way. Consider Rick your personal coach. In addition, *Crunch Time* shares the performance-under-pressure secrets gathered from my interviews with a number of other elite leaders, coaches, and performers. If you're a baseball fan, you'll recognize Oakland A's General Manager Billy Beane of *Moneyball* fame, Hall of Famer Tom Glavine, Cy Young Award winner Barry Zito, and the inspirational Olympic hero Jim Abbott. I also tap into the wisdom of elite performers outside of baseball, including CEOs, executive coaches, leadership guru Ken Blanchard, and award-wining Director Stephen Soderbergh. Rick and I are fortunate to call these individuals our friends.

While *Crunch Time* shares a number of entertaining, behind-the-scenes stories from Rick's career in baseball, you don't need to be a baseball fan to find this book enjoyable and valuable. The lessons shared transcend baseball, applying to the everyday pressure situations you face.

Furthermore, the lessons shared by the elite leaders, coaches, and performers are not just for the elite; they are relevant and valuable for everyone. Throughout the book, I share how I've applied what I've learned and the resulting fruit from the shifts in my thinking.

For example, in 2015, my first full year of consciously reframing pressure situations from threat to opportunity, the annual sales revenue I am responsible for increased 25 percent! The customers my teammates and I serve also achieved great outcomes. Based on these results and how they were achieved, I earned a promotion to Vice President. In this new role, I have more responsibility, more pressure, and more opportunity to expand my influence and impact.

Here's one quick piece of advice before you dive in: read the Introduction, Chapter 1, and Chapter 2 in order. These serve as the foundation for the rest of the book. Following Chapter 2, you may choose to read Chapters 3–8 in whatever sequence suits you best.

—*Judd Hoekstra*

Foreword

I t's well documented in *Moneyball* that we (the Oakland A's of the late 1990s and early 2000s) were going to great lengths to rethink all aspects of baseball: how it is managed, how it is played, who is best suited to play it, and why.

The gap between the rich and the poor was growing wider than ever. To some, especially baseball traditionalists, having the second lowest payroll in baseball might be viewed as a threat. A threat to landing talent. A threat to winning. A threat to keeping our jobs. For us, it was the opposite; it was liberating. We could break the rules and take chances bigger payroll teams wouldn't dream of taking. It gave us the opportunity to explore new frontiers in every area of the game.

I knew bringing Rick Peterson onboard as our pitching coach represented tremendous growth for us and would give us an edge. Rick is anything but your typical baseball guy. He's an educated guy who studied psychology and art in college. He is very intellectually curious. We were the same. It was a great match in our minds.

Rick was always looking to learn and was going to explore every possible way to make our pitchers not only better, but also healthier. When we were together, Rick was looking into areas no other coaches were looking at—biomechanical analysis with Dr. James Andrews, statistical probabilities associated with various pitch counts, sports psychology, and even mindfulness—to figure out how to improve our pitchers' performance.

What strikes me about Rick is just how open he is to new ideas, to challenging traditional thinking. That's what reframing is all about—choosing to see the world through a different lens that enables you to bring out the best in yourself and others.

Rick reframed how to best achieve maximum pitching performance, especially in pressure situations. He showed that performing in the clutch is not a case of "you have it or you don't." Rather, it can be learned.

He successfully brought out the best in the budding young stars of our pitching staff—the Big Three of Barry Zito, Tim Hudson, and Mark Mulder. Perhaps even more importantly, he helped the other less-physically-gifted pitchers like Chad Bradford and Cory Lidle maximize their potential and their contributions to our team. Baseball is a game with razor-thin margins of victory. Being able to get all your players—from the top of your roster to the bottom—to consistently perform to their potential in pressure situations is frequently the difference between winning and losing.

Throughout my career, both as a player and an executive, I've clearly seen differences in how some players cave under the pressure while others thrive. With entertaining stories from an insider's perspective, Rick and Judd share how those who appear to be immune to the pressure think differently and are able to be their best when it matters most.

Just as Rick was a difference-maker for our team, the wisdom captured in *Crunch Time* will be a difference-maker for you and your team. Enjoy!

> —*Billy Beane, Executive Vice President of Baseball Operations, Oakland Athletics*

CRUNCH TIME

HOW TO BE YOUR **BEST** WHEN IT MATTERS **MOST**

INTRODUCTION

Rick and Izzy

Baseball is 90 percent mental. The other half is physical.

—*YOGI BERRA*

It's October 11, 2001, and the Oakland A's are playing the New York Yankees in Game 2 of the opening round of the American League Playoffs. Nearly 57,000 raucous fans are in attendance at Yankee Stadium, with a TV audience of 11 million.

Tim Hudson, the A's starting pitcher, has been nothing less than brilliant. He's staked the A's to a 2–0 lead. But it's the bottom of the 9th inning, and the situation for Oakland grows particularly nerve-racking. Hudson no longer pitches. On the mound, trying to finish the game, is the A's closer, Jason "Izzy" Isringhausen.

Last season, in his first full season as a closer, Izzy made the American League All-Star team. He showed he clearly had the physical talent to succeed. But that season wasn't without its rocky moments. Facing these same Yankees on August 8, 2000, Izzy blew the game by giving up back-to-back 9th inning home runs to Bernie Williams and David Justice.

This season, Izzy has struggled and his confidence has plummeted. By the start of August, he had nine blown saves. At one point in the season, he had been temporarily removed from his closer's role to give him a break and try to get him back on track. As you would expect, fear, worry, and doubt invaded Izzy's mind.

The bottom of the 9th inning starts with Izzy surrendering a leadoff double to Williams. Izzy then walks Tino Martinez on five pitches to put runners at first and second with nobody out. Izzy sees Jorge Posada confidently striding to the plate. He looks at the on-deck circle and sees Justice. Both players appear excited about the opportunity to get to Izzy and win the game for the Yankees in dramatic fashion.

This is a crisis.

Despite his 6-foot 3-inch, 210-pound frame, Izzy is currently anything but intimidating. He kicks at the pitching rubber distractedly as he turns the baseball over and over in his right hand, looking for the perfect spot to grip. He grimaces and rapidly chomps on his gum. He seems hesitant, unsure of himself.

From the A's dugout comes the cry of "Time!" Out steps the A's pitching coach, Rick Peterson. His appearance elicits jeers from the hostile Bronx crowd. Peterson, nicknamed "The Professor" for his scientific approach to pitching, jogs quickly to the mound as if he has something important to share with Izzy. Peterson smiles, puts his hand on Izzy's shoulder, and begins to talk as if they are the only two people in the ballpark. Izzy laughs, then nods. He straightens up and seems more confident, more relaxed. Peterson quickly returns to the dugout, his conversation with Izzy taking less than a minute.

Izzy turns his attention back to the batter's box. He bends at the waist, dangles his arm by his side, and locks in on the catcher's sign. Izzy nods his head with confidence and begins delivering his pitches like a new man. In rapid succession, he strikes out Posada, induces Justice to pop out to the third baseman, and jams former playoff-hero Scott Brosius, who pops harmlessly to the first baseman to end the game. Crisis averted. Izzy comes through in this nail-biter. The A's win.

While the outcome is known, questions remain about how Izzy quickly regained his composure and came through in the clutch.

What exactly did Rick say? Did he correct a technical flaw in Izzy's mechanics? No.

Stay tuned. We'll tell you what happened at the end of this introduction.

Pressure to Perform

In today's hypercompetitive world, we all face significant pressure to perform. In the business world, these pressures come in many forms, including, but not limited to, urgent project deadlines, stretch goals, sales presentations and negotiations with millions of dollars on the line, question and answer sessions with a challenging audience, tough feedback from your boss, job interviews, and the ever-increasing mantra to "do more with less." At school, pressures can come in the form of heavy workloads, exams, and the social desire to fit in. Whether it's a dance competition, a piano recital, or a baseball game, even our recreation is filled with pressure.

For example, the pressures I'm currently facing include these:

- Navigating the interviews, research, writing, and deadlines associated with this book

- Investing the 60 or more hours a week I work in my day job to make a positive difference in the lives of our customers and the people I lead

- Serving as a loving husband

- Acting as a positive role model to my two teenagers

- Proactively managing my Type 1 diabetes to stay healthy

We are all challenged by countless high-pressure situations in our daily lives. Like Izzy, we want to perform our best when it matters most. But something happens when the pressure rises; in retrospect, we know we performed far below our capabilities.

I will soon dive into the reasons for this dreaded truth. For now, let's just say that, in too many cases, we get in our own way and sabotage our performance. Across every profession and walk of life, failing under pressure continues to plague performers. It doesn't need to be this way. Rick and I can help.

Think of Rick as your personal coach. He will coach you to *reframe*—a cognitive skill you can use to quickly and effectively equip your mind and body to perform well under pressure, anytime, anywhere.

I have two roles in this book: first, to share Rick's and others' wisdom in a fun, entertaining way that also gives you a behind-the-scenes look into the world of elite performers under pressure; second, to show you how I've applied what Rick and others have taught me to my professional and personal life. As I do so, you will see that reframing is not just for professional athletes, coaches, and CEOs. It's for all of us.

What Separates the Best from the Rest at Crunch Time?

Rick's and my experience and interviews with elite performers reveal that, even more than physical skills, it's performers' mindsets that separate the best from the rest under pressure. Clutch performers know how to think on command in ways that help, rather than harm, their performance. Thinking differently is the starting point. Change how you act, and change your results.

Thoughts & Emotions → Actions → Results

Once you get to the highest level, everyone has talent. They have the physical tools. The mental side of it is what really sets you apart and allows your talent to come through.

—*Barry Zito, 2002 Cy Young Award winner with the Oakland A's*

So How Did Rick Help Izzy Get Out of the Jam?

Let's get back to the story of Rick and Izzy in the bottom of the 9th inning. As Rick stood on the mound with his hand on Izzy's shoulder, Rick could feel Izzy's body shaking.

> Izzy mumbled anxiously,
> "I can't feel my legs."
>
> The pitching coach smiled and responded,
> "That's okay; we don't need you to kick a field goal."

The humor served as an open valve, releasing Izzy's pressure. The humor also opened up Izzy's mind so it was receptive to a new thought, which Rick then provided.

Rick continued, telling Izzy that in a situation like they were in, nerves were to be expected, but those nerves didn't need to get in the way of executing the task at hand. Rick directed Izzy to focus on the simple task he'd executed to perfection thousands of times before.

> "Hit the (catcher's) glove! Remember, you're a professional glove hitter!"

The nerves and the task could coexist nicely, with no diminishment in performance. Free from fear, worry, doubt, and a multitude of mental distractions, Izzy repeated to himself, "Hit the glove!" Based on his rapid change in demeanor and his superb performance, clearly Izzy took his coach's advice to heart.

Rick helped Izzy out of the jam by *reframing*.

1

Reframing—The Shortest Path from Threat to Opportunity

If opportunity doesn't knock, build a door.

—*MILTON BERLE*

At its core, reframing describes the *skill* of consciously and intentionally thinking about a situation in a new or different way. This, in turn, allows us to shift the meaning we attach to the situation, the actions we take, and the results we achieve. The operative word in our definition is *skill.* In other words, it's not something some are gifted with and others are not. With practice, reframing can be learned by anyone.

Blanchard Executive Coach Kate Larsen shared the following analogy with me to describe how reframing works.[1] You hop into your car and start the engine. The radio is already on and is playing a song on one of your preset stations. The song is like the voice in your head (a.k.a. your self-talk),

> **reframe** [riːˈfreɪm]
>
> *The skill of consciously thinking about a situation in a new or different way to change how you interpret the situation, the actions you take, and the results you achieve*

often filled with emotion. The preset station is the equivalent of a long-held assumption or belief.

The volume is low and you may not be paying attention to what's playing. It's just on in the background as you drive and think about other things. Then you decide to turn up the volume. Now you are aware of the song that's playing. Let's assume, in this case, the song is one you do not like. Being aware of the song you don't like is the equivalent of consciously paying attention to your negative self-talk.

You now have a choice. You can keep listening to the song and let it affect your thoughts and your emotions. Or you can check out what else is playing by changing the station. Changing the station to identify better songs is the equivalent of identifying different and better thoughts that are likely to lead to better actions and better outcomes.

Taking this analogy one step further, we used to live in a world where, based on the number of radio stations we could access, we were limited in the songs we could choose. Sometimes, no matter how hard we tried, we just couldn't find a song we liked on the radio. We no longer live in that world. We live in a world where we can create custom playlists loaded with our favorite songs for every occasion. In a similar fashion, Chapters 3–8 provide a playlist of reframes you can use to be your best at crunch time.

It's important to highlight that reframing is not about pretending everything is perfect and positive. It is about finding different ways of interpreting a less-than-ideal situation. The resulting new frame leads to a different meaning, which leads to better actions and better results. Just as important, you feel better about how you handle the situation.

The skill of reframing is useful for many situations—in particular those in which you feel an uncomfortable degree of pressure, anxiety, or stress. Here are a few examples.

1. In the late 1980s, a parasitic insect named phylloxera threatened to destroy vineyards and bring Napa Valley wineries to their knees. The projected cost of replanting the grapes was $25,000 to $75,000 an acre. This didn't even take into account the opportunity cost of a five-year wait for new vines to bear fruit.

   In spite of the financial and time investment costs, a few growers did replant. One of those growers, Jack Cakebread at Cakebread Cellars, recalls, "Phylloxera was the greatest opportunity the valley has ever had. It was an *unbelievable opportunity*![2]

   "How often in your life do you get a chance to go back and say, 'Hey, if I had this to do over again, I'd do it this way'? We had all the new technology. We had root stocks. We had clones of varieties you are looking at now. We had spacing. We had soil analysis we never had before. It was just a dream!"

   Cakebread Cellars, producer of 75,000 cases of wine per year, is now one of the most highly esteemed and successful wineries in Napa Valley. Where others saw despair, Jack Cakebread saw hope. He saw the chance to start anew.

2. During the Korean War, the Chinese communists had overrun the Yalu River. The Marines battling the Chinese were in a running fight to reach the coast. Ten Chinese divisions surrounded Colonel Lewis Burwell Puller's 1st Marines. The unyielding Colonel saw the dire situation from a unique perspective: "Those poor bastards," Puller said. "They've got us right where we want them. We can fire in any direction now!"

3. When President Ronald Reagan was running for reelection in 1984, he was the oldest president to have ever served. At

age 73, there were many questions about Reagan's capacity to endure the grueling demands of the presidency. On October 7, Reagan performed poorly in the first debate against his opponent, Democratic candidate Walter Mondale. Among other mistakes, Reagan admitted to being "confused."

Two weeks later, in the next debate, Mondale made a comment that implied Reagan's advanced age was an issue voters should be concerned about. Reagan's comeback was priceless. He joked, "I will not make age an issue of this campaign. I am not going to exploit, for political purposes, my opponent's youth and inexperience." Mondale himself laughed at Reagan's joke. With that humorous reframe, Reagan effectively neutralized the age issue, ended Mondale's campaign, and steamrolled to reelection.

In each of these examples, where it might be natural to feel overwhelmed and threatened, these individuals saw opportunity.

While reframing can be used in a variety of contexts, this book focuses on helping you perform your best under pressure. On that note, I want to make an important point; you need to calibrate your expectations with reality. It is unrealistic to expect to perform better under pressure than you perform under calm conditions. As a result, *your goal under pressure is to perform at a level equal to how you typically perform when there is no pressure.*

Seven Reasons Reframing Is Priceless

Let's have a look at seven reasons why reframing is an incredibly valuable skill.

1. As I stated earlier, reframing is a skill that, with practice, **can be learned**.

2. In today's world, it can be argued that time is our most valuable resource. While the 10,000-hour rule to master a new skill is true for many skills, who has 10,000 hours to spare? We're constantly on the lookout for life hacks—tricks that not only produce great results, but do so in record time. Reframing is **as quick as coming up with a new thought**, which can be measured in seconds.

3. In addition to being fast, reframing is **efficient**. It redirects your attention toward the opportunity before you rather than toward what could go wrong. This enables you to use your energy wisely.

4. Unlike dunking a basketball or becoming a supermodel, reframing is not limited to those who have won the genetic lottery. Reframing also knows no economic boundaries. It can and has been used by the extremely rich, the extremely poor, and everyone in between. Reframing is **available to everyone**.

5. Also, to reframe, we don't need to be in the office, or in front of our laptops or smart phones, or on a practice field. We can reframe while we're driving, talking a walk, mowing the lawn, and so on. Because the skill resides in our mind, reframing **can help you anytime, anywhere**.

6. Reframing **applies in all different types of pressure situations**. It applies at work as you seek to solve problems, make presentations, or beat your quota. It applies in academics as you take exams. It applies in your personal life as you sing a solo in the church choir or play in a big game.

7. In addition to being a skill you can use to help yourself, reframing is a key skill you can use to **teach and positively influence others**. When Martin Luther King, Jr. spoke at

the March on Washington in 1963 and gave his famous "I Have a Dream" speech, he reframed the civil rights movement from a struggle of mighty proportions to an inspiring dream embraced by many.

Now that we have shared examples and you know more about reframing, let's shift to understanding how pressure affects your mind and body.

How Does Pressure Affect Your Mind and Body?

When we're under pressure, we can think about the situation in one of two ways—either as a *threat* or as an *opportunity*.

Whether you view the situation as a threat or opportunity depends on how you answer this question for yourself: *"Do I have what it takes to handle this situation?"*

When you answer *"no,"* you view the situation as a threat. The perception of pressure situations as a threat hurts our performance. *Why?* With threat thinking, your mind is typically filled with thoughts and feelings that

- You have little to no control over the situation.

- You're filled with anxiety, fear, worry, and doubt.

- You're focused on trying to avoid failure and its devastating consequences.

These thoughts and emotions, in turn, trigger responses we're all familiar with: butterflies in your stomach, sweaty palms, dry mouth and throat, and tense muscles, to name a few. In addition, threat thinking leads to an increased heart rate and the production of performance-crippling chemicals such as cortisol—a.k.a. the stress hormone. In heavy doses triggered by threat, cortisol causes your blood vessels to constrict, limiting the amount of oxygen and glucose that reach your muscles and brain. This, in turn, compromises your ability to make good decisions and perform at the level you're capable of under less stressful conditions.

Before Rick's visit to the mound in the bottom of the 9th inning, Izzy felt—in a word—threatened.

In contrast, when you answer *"yes"* to the question *"Do I have what it takes to handle this?"* you view the situation as an opportunity. With opportunity thinking, your mind is typically filled with thoughts and feelings that

- You're in control.

- You're confident.

- You're focused on the success you view as being within your grasp.

These thoughts and emotions, in turn, trigger a performance-enhancing response from your body's internal pharmacy. Like threat thinking, opportunity thinking also causes your body to respond with an increased heart rate. However, unlike threat thinking that releases cortisol in large amounts that hinder us, opportunity thinking releases dopamine, the feel-good neurotransmitter.

Dopamine causes your blood vessels to dilate, increasing the amount of oxygen and glucose getting to your muscles and brain. This, in turn, helps you make good decisions and perform at the level you're capable of under normal conditions.

Learning the skill to get yourself into opportunity thinking for pressure situations is critical for performing your best. *After* Rick's visit to the mound in the bottom of the 9th inning, Izzy saw the opportunity.

In essence, your mind is filled with beliefs that can either hurt you or help you. These beliefs, in turn, spark an internal pharmacy within your body that releases chemicals that can also hurt you or help you.

The Mind-Body Connection

Consider the following well-known example to illustrate the point that your mind and body are inextricably linked.

Task 1 Imagine you are asked to walk 50 yards on a bridge. The bridge is the width of a sidewalk, has no guard rails, and is 1 foot off the ground. What thoughts are going through your head? How does your body feel? How likely are you to succeed? What are the consequences if you fail? How important is this task to you?

Task 2 Now imagine you are asked to walk 50 yards on a bridge that is the width of a sidewalk and has no guard rails. This time, however, the bridge is 1,000 feet in the air, over a stadium full of people. What thoughts are going through your head? How does your body feel? How likely are you to succeed? What are the consequences if you fail? How important is this task to you?

In both tasks, the physical requirements of you are the same—walk 50 yards on a bridge that is the width of a sidewalk and has no guard rails. However, you likely had very different inner reactions to the tasks in terms of the thoughts that went through your head and how your body felt. The reason you had different reactions to the task is due to the significant difference in the consequences of failure between the two tasks. There is little to no pressure in Task 1, and you likely have a high degree of confidence you will succeed. With Task 2, however, the dire consequences of failure lead to threat thinking. Confidence likely wanes and your focus shifts from the act of walking on the sidewalk to falling down from 1,000 feet in the air.

As you can see from this simple example, it's not the physical requirements of a task that cause us to feel threatened. Rather, *it's **our perception** of the requirements that cause us to feel threatened.*

Most often, pressure comes from within, not from others. Consequently, the best response also comes from within—by learning how to modify our thinking. The answer is learning how to reframe.

Highlights

- Our experience and interviews with elite performers reveal that, even more than physical skills, it's performers' mindsets that separate the best from the rest. The most clutch performers know how to think on command when under pressure, and in ways that optimize their performance.

- Reframing describes the *skill* of deliberately thinking about a situation in a new or different way. This, in turn, allows us to shift the meaning we attach to the situation, the actions we take, and the results we achieve.

- When we're under pressure, we can think about the situation in one of two ways—either as a *threat* or as an *opportunity*. Seeing the pressure situation as a threat triggers the bad pharmacy in our body and hurts our performance. Seeing the pressure situation as an opportunity triggers the good pharmacy in our body and helps our performance.

- Like Izzy, we all want to come through at crunch time.

Try This

- Identify a high-pressure situation you're facing now or will be facing in the near future (e.g., completing a big project with an impending deadline, making an important presentation to a challenging audience, performing in a game or a recital, taking a final exam). Use this situation as the context for practicing the skill of reframing as you read this book.

- Write down what you're currently thinking and feeling about your high-pressure situation.

- Are you seeing it as a threat or an opportunity? If a threat, come up with two ways to think about it as an opportunity.

- If you can already see the opportunity, write that down.

While you may be ready to acknowledge the value of reframing, you may be wondering why it's so critical to use this skill in pressure-packed situations. Let's find out.

2

Why Reframing at Crunch Time Is Necessary

There is one thing I know. Never ever in history has panic ever solved anything. It's literally never happened.[1]

—*STEVEN SODERBERGH, Palme d'Or winner at the Cannes Film Festival, Academy Award winner for Best Director*

Our brains are magnificent and powerful organs with ultra-fast processing speeds. A team of researchers using the fourth fastest supercomputer in the world—the K computer at the Riken research institute in Kobe, Japan—simulated one second of human brain activity. They did so by creating an artificial neural network of 1.73 billion nerve cells connected by 10.4 trillion synapses. While this is impressive, the researchers were not able to simulate the brain's activity in real time. In fact, it took *40 minutes* with the combined muscle of *82,944 processors* in the K computer to get just *1 second of biological brain processing time.*[2]

In order to operate at this breakneck speed, your brain uses short-cuts. It reflexively assesses a situation and tries to make meaning.

One such shortcut is our instinctual fight, flight, or freeze response in the face of a perceived threat. Consider a situation where you are being chased down the street by the neighborhood pit bull. Your brain signals danger. Your brain then floods your body with chemical impulses that tell your body to fight, flee, or freeze. All of this happens in an instant, without your conscious thought.

While our fight, flight, or freeze reflexive reaction serves as valuable protection to physical threats, it's not relevant when applied to most modern-day pressure situations. Public speaking, for example, is not an imminent threat to your physical safety even though it might feel as if you're going to die from doing it. But in our mind's eye, we perceive a pressure situation as a threat or as an opportunity. Viewing pressure as a threat harms our performance. Unfortunately, our reflexive reaction to pressure is threat.

> **reflexive** [ree-flek-siv]
>
> *A spontaneous reaction made without conscious thought*

How Our Mind Works Under Pressure

To learn about why our reflexive reaction to pressure is threat, we need to understand some basics about how the human brain works. Our goal is not to turn you into a neuroscientist. Instead, we will translate the science of the brain into simple and practical terms.

When you have an easy-to-understand, working model of your brain, you can begin to use this knowledge to your benefit. Our goal is for you to apply these teachings in your own life—to override your primal, reflexive reaction to pressure and consciously choose a different, performance-enhancing response.

If we look at how our mind operates under pressure, it's helpful to consider three key regions of the brain and how scientists and psychologists can help us understand the mechanics of how we handle pressure.[3]

- The Caveman (a.k.a. the reptilian complex)
- The Conscious Thinker (a.k.a. the neocortex)
- The Hard Drive (a.k.a. the limbic system)

The Caveman (applicable to both men and women; I'll use Caveman throughout for simplicity's sake) lives in the brain stem and cerebellum. It is the threat center of your brain. The Caveman's goal is simple—to survive. It is constantly on patrol, looking for danger. When faced with a threat, the Caveman's instantaneous reaction is fight, flight, or freeze. This reaction is the Caveman's most frequently used and most important instinct.

In prehistoric times, when many threats were physical in nature, the Caveman's fight, flight, or freeze reaction served as a successful survival response. By natural selection, the people with the fastest and strongest Caveman had the highest survival rate.

Tens of thousands of years later, the Caveman part of our brain's operating system is alive and strong as ever. However, with today's world being so very different from the prehistoric world, the Caveman isn't as valuable as it used to be. Most of the pressure situations we face in the modern world don't involve a physical threat. Instead, our threats are typically psychological in nature. However, our Caveman does not distinguish between today's *psychological* threats and prehistoric *physical* threats. It reacts the same way to speaking in front of others and being judged as it does to being chased by the neighborhood pit bull. The blood rushes to our limbs to get us ready to run or punch; when this happens, the blood is rushing away from our brains! Our capacity to think clearly is restricted.

As a result, our Caveman's fight, flight, or freeze reflexive reaction doesn't help us with psychological threats. In fact, this reflexive reaction hurts us. The very strength of the Caveman in prehistoric times turns out to be a huge crippler of performance under modern-day pressure.

Let's look more specifically at how the Caveman reacts to modern-day pressures.

- It fixates on what could go wrong and is consumed by fear, worry, and doubt.

- It quickly forms an opinion based on feelings, not facts, and then seeks information that supports its opinion.

- It lacks perspective, exaggerating the importance of a situation.

- It fails to see options, thinking in terms of absolutes, do-or-die.

- It exaggerates the likelihood of a poor outcome.

- It exaggerates the consequences of failure.

- It is insecure and highly concerned with others' judgment.

- It personalizes failure.

For modern-day pressures, whether it's a critical business presentation, an academic test, an athletic performance, or a piano recital, letting your Caveman take over is a bad idea. Daniel Goleman, author of the bestseller *Emotional Intelligence*, coined the term *amygdala hijack* to describe "emotional responses from people which are immediate and overwhelming, and out of measure with the actual stimulus because it has triggered a much more significant emotional threat."[4]

How do we know when we've been hijacked by our Caveman? It's emotional and irrational reaction typically results in negative self-talk:

Why am I doing this? This is a stupid idea. There's no way I can do this. The people I'm competing against are so much better than me. What if this goes wrong? What if I make a bad decision? I can't handle this. Is there any way for me to get out of this? This is the most important presentation/game/performance I've ever had. I'll never get another opportunity like this again. I have no choice. I must succeed/win. If I screw this up, it'll be devastating. I won't be able to show my face around here ever again. This is a nightmare. I'm terrible under pressure. There are a lot of people watching me. They will think I'm an idiot. They will laugh at me. My teammates will be so disappointed in me. I am a total failure.

What would you think of me if I talked to you the way you talk to yourself? You'd think I was a jerk. You have no right to be your own worst coach.

—Rick Peterson

If we put a speaker on your thoughts and broadcast what you say to yourself, we would institutionalize you. You wouldn't hang out with people who talk to you the way you talk to yourself. *So why do we talk to ourselves this way?*

It isn't really you talking. It's your Caveman. This is a very important point and distinction.

> ## While your Caveman lives in your brain, it's not really you.

By allowing you to understand that these instinctual, primal pressure reactions are from your Caveman and not from you, we hope to enable you to stop beating yourself up for having these thoughts and emotions.[5]

So If the Caveman isn't really you, who are you? The part of your brain you *want* to activate under pressure is the Conscious Thinker.

It lives in the neocortex of your brain. While the Caveman's goal is to survive, your goal as the Conscious Thinker is to thrive.

Based on this goal, let's look more specifically at the winning beliefs of you, the Conscious Thinker, under pressure.

- You see pressure as a challenge, an opportunity to demonstrate your skills.
- You are filled with confidence.
- You are focused only on what you can control.
- You are focused on performing to your capabilities, doing *your* best.
- You perform for yourself, not for others.
- Your self-esteem is based on your intrinsic worth, not on your performance or the opinion of others.
- You search out facts before reaching a conclusion.
- You see the big picture and keep the situation in proper perspective.
- You explore options.
- You have an objective view of the likelihood of a given outcome.
- You know you can deal with the consequences of any outcome.
- You learn from less than ideal outcomes.

As you'd expect, the self-talk from your Conscious Thinker is much more helpful.

I am performing because I enjoy it and it helps me reach my goals. I know I can do this because

> **conscious**
>
> [kon-shuh s]
>
> *Fully aware, deliberate, and intentional*

of the skills I've acquired during my practice and preparation. I don't expect to be perfect. I expect to do my best and perform like I have in practice. While I would like to succeed/win, I understand I am not in control of all the factors impacting the outcome. Because I've given my best, I can live with any outcome. I am focused on being my best, not on concerning myself with what others think of me. That's out of my control. Regardless of the outcome, I will have other opportunities in the future to demonstrate my skills.

Your Conscious Thinker is where choice lives. Even though it's not always easy, it's critical to remember...

In every moment, we can *choose* our thoughts.

Based on the descriptions of how the Caveman thinks and how you think, it's easy to see pressure situations create a battle for control of your mind. Unfortunately, in this fight, the Caveman has a couple of unfair advantages.

The Caveman is faster. According to Dr. Evian Gordon, a neuroscientist who specializes in high performance, five times each second the brain non-consciously determines what is dangerous and steers away from it.[6] In every situation, before any input has a chance to reach the Conscious Thinker, it goes to your Caveman first. You can't change this. In situations where physical danger is present and a fight, flight, or freeze reaction is warranted, this could actually save your life. However, in situations where the perceived danger is psychological, as most modern-day pressures are, the Caveman's reaction is not helpful.

The Neuro-Leadership scientist David Rock explains the threat response "is mentally taxing and deadly to the productivity of a person... [The threat response] impairs analytical thinking, creative

25

insight and problem solving." As a result, it's a good idea to understand and avoid triggering your threat response.[7]

In addition to being faster, the Caveman is stronger. Many more of the neural pathways in our brain are devoted to danger and threat detection than to reward detection.[8] As a result, it's easy to see why fear, worry, and doubt are so deeply embedded in our operating systems.

So how do you know when your Caveman has hijacked your thinking? Dr. Steve Peters, author of *The Chimp Paradox* and an English psychiatrist who works in elite sport, says the easiest way is to ask yourself,

Do I want to think or feel this way?

Quite simply, if the answer is no, then your Caveman is in control.

You're probably thinking, *"I should just get rid of my Caveman."* As I learned about how the brain functions, I had the same thought. And while surgery to remove your amygdala would likely improve your performance under pressure, it would leave you with some very undesirable side effects. For one, you would lose your fight, flight, or freeze instinct that protects you from legitimate physical threats. Second, without an amygdala, you would be void of emotion. You'd miss out on life's joyous moments, some of which include performing your best under pressure.

So, if we can't get rid of our Caveman, what are we to do? We need to learn to tame our Caveman. But first, let's look at the third part of our brain which is useful in understanding how we think under pressure.

Your Hard Drive resides in the limbic system of your brain. It stores your values, memories, and beliefs and uses these to decide how to act. The Caveman saves to your Hard Drive values, memories, and beliefs based on emotion. Your Conscious Thinker saves to your Hard Drive values, memories, and beliefs based on logic.

Just like a real computer, your Hard Drive doesn't know the quality of the data you put into it. It simply acts on the data it is given. In the case of the Caveman, you're left with the old saying, "garbage in, garbage out." The opposite is true as well. The more your Hard Drive contains values, beliefs, and memories from your Conscious Thinker, the better your decisions and actions under pressure will be.

We readily acknowledge this is an overly simplistic view of what's really a very complicated process going on in our brains. Again, our goal is not to turn you into a neuroscientist; it is to give you a model of your mind under pressure that you can understand and apply.

Now that I know how my brain works under pressure, what's next? In order to perform your best in the clutch, you need to learn to tame your Caveman and download more of your Conscious Thinker's values, beliefs, and memories onto your Hard Drive. This requires you to use the skill of *reframing*.

You need to override the reflexive frame your Caveman presents to you under pressure and choose the better frame of your Conscious Thinker. To do this, you need to create space and time.

Create Space and Time

The following is an analogy from the game of hockey I was reminded of by Brian Hennessy, a customer and fellow hockey coach. For years I've coached kids carrying the puck into the offensive zone to skate into an open space. When you're carrying the puck and a defender pressures you by taking away your space and time, you're likely to make a poor decision. In contrast, when you can curl away from a defender and get to open space on the ice, you have time to survey the play and make a good decision. The time and space gives you time for quick reflection, allowing you to see things you wouldn't otherwise see.

The same happens in our lives when we are under pressure and are triggered into an emotional reaction. If we can just create space and time, we can survey the situation and make a better choice. We can see things we would otherwise miss. It gives us a chance to allow our Conscious Thinker to get in the game.

Reframing Cole's Hockey Tryout

To continue with the hockey theme, I will share a personal story of managing my Caveman's reflexive reaction and bringing my Conscious Thinker into the game. It's September 1, 2015, the first night of hockey tryouts for my then 12-year-old son, Cole. He's trying out for a club he's not played with in the past. He's skated with 25 kids all summer who are competing for 17 roster spots. At the conclusion of tryouts, there will be some heartbroken kids who get cut.

When we show up at the ice rink for the first night of tryouts, Cole is handed a white tryout jersey with a black number 28 on the back so he can be identified by the coaches who are evaluating the players.

My wife Sherry and I settle into our seats among other parents to watch the tryout. Based on what I've learned and shared with Cole about reframing pressure, I'm hopeful he will remain poised and will demonstrate his skills.

The kids are separated into two teams, one with black-colored jerseys and the other with white-colored jerseys. As the kids go through the typical pre-game warm-up routine that includes shooting on the goalies, my wife and I quickly notice many of the most skilled players are wearing black jerseys. It's a good bet the kids on the black team have already secured roster spots. It's not lost on either of us that Cole is on the white team.

When the scrimmage begins, the black team quickly asserts its dominance. The white team is overmatched. To say fear, worry, and doubt creep into our minds is an understatement.

Sherry voices her fears to me. "This is really bad. It's so unfair. Why would the coach set up the teams to be so uneven? Maybe we shouldn't even have him go to tomorrow night's tryouts (when the team's roster is chosen). I can't stand seeing Cole get hurt. Let's just go back to the team he played with last year." Truth be told, the initial reaction from my Caveman is just as strong as Sherry's reaction. The only difference between Sherry's reaction and my reaction is I don't say out loud what my Caveman is thinking.

Because I've been immersed for the past couple years in the topic of reframing pressure from threat to opportunity, I recognize this as the perfect time to use this skill. I start by pausing and recognizing what Sherry has voiced and what my Caveman is saying to me. Once I realize I don't want to think or feel this way, I start asking questions to challenge my Caveman. Instead of assuming the worst—everyone wearing a white jersey will be cut from the team—I ask questions and look for different ways to interpret the facts of the situation.

I ask, *"Why might the coach set up the teams this way?"* *"What is he trying to evaluate in such a lopsided scenario?"* As a former coach who has been through the tryout process on multiple occasions, I think this coach might be trying to evaluate a small number of players on the white team in the toughest circumstances possible. If a player on the white team can perform well against a team full of highly skilled players, then he's likely to perform even better if he plays on the same post-tryout team as these highly skilled players.

Then, being as objective as possible, I ask, *"How is Cole performing?"* As I watch Cole play, I notice him performing well and demonstrating his skills in a variety of difficult situations. He isn't perfect, but that's an unrealistic expectation for him. In the course of an hour of play, no 12-year-old hockey player is flawless.

I share my reframed thinking with Sherry and both of us are able to calm our minds. More importantly, as parents, this allows us to have a calm, rational conversation with Cole following the tryout. On the car ride home from the rink, I want to know how Cole is feeling about the first night of tryouts. I ask him, "How do you think you played tonight?"

Cole responds calmly, "I think I played pretty well. It was tough out there because the other team had most of the best guys, but I think that's the way coach wanted it so he could see how the rest of us played against the toughest competition possible." Either the coach let the kids know this or Cole did some reframing of his own to keep himself calm. I don't let Cole know it took me longer than it took him to come to this same effective and objective interpretation of the situation. The next night, we receive the fun news that Cole made the team. Reframing pressure—even a 12-year-old hockey player can do it!

Fast-forward to March 13, 2016. Cole and his team finish a great season by winning the Illinois AA state championship. During the celebration, I pause to think about how Cole might have missed out on this memorable season if he hadn't known how to reframe the threat he faced during tryouts.

The Steps to Reframing

For those readers who value a process-oriented approach, here is a quick look at the steps I used to reframe my thinking about Cole's hockey tryout.

1. **Pause and Recognize Your Caveman's Story.** Pay attention to your reflexive self-talk—the story your Caveman is telling you. Ask yourself, *"Do I want to think, feel, or act this way?"*

   Remember, you cannot stop the reflexive *reaction* to a pressure situation by the Caveman. However, you can stop the Caveman from *acting* on this reflexive reaction. It's important to recognize our Caveman presents its reflexive thinking as a command. In reality, it is not a command. It is merely an offer to your Conscious Thinker to act in a certain way. The choice about how you will think and act belongs to your Conscious Thinker.[9]

2. **Challenge Your Caveman's Story.** Question the most seemingly unassailable beliefs and assumptions. Remember, your brain is like a computer. It doesn't know the difference between the truth and a lie. It just responds to what you fill it with. If your Hard Drive is filled with bad beliefs and assumptions (note: we all have them), it will produce a bad result. Garbage in, garbage out.

When Garry Ridge, Hall of Fame reframer and WD-40 Company CEO, faces a pressure situation, he pauses and asks himself why he thinks and feels the way he does.[10] More specifically, he asks himself:

- What assumptions am I making in this situation?
- What's driving these assumptions—fact, fiction, or opinion?
- What am I afraid of?

We'll learn more about reframing from Garry in Chapter 7, including the fabulous results achieved by WD-40 Company.

Don't let the force of an impression when it first hit[s] you knock you off your feet; just say to it: Hold on a moment; let me see who you are and what you represent. Let me put you to the test.

—*Epictetus*

---

3. **Explore Different, Rational Stories**. Identify at least two different ways of viewing the current situation. Ask yourself questions to open up your mind to possibilities:

- *How else can I think about this?*

- *Where can I find humor in this?*

- *How might <insert name of person you admire and respect> think about this?* [11]

- *What would I tell my kids to do in this situation?*

- *What would I do if I weren't afraid?* Note: Facebook stamps this question on bold colored posters throughout its facilities, reminding employees daily to move from threat to opportunity.

If you are stuck and can't come up with alternatives on your own, ask those around you to share how they view the situation.

4. **Choose and Act on Your Best New Story**. Choose the story that most increases your sense of control, confidence, and vision of success. Remember, fill your Hard Drive with thoughts and beliefs that come from you, the Conscious Thinker.

By overriding the reflexive thoughts that aren't helping us with new thoughts that do help us, we can move from experiencing pressure as a threat to perceiving it as an opportunity. The more we flex this new muscle, the more it becomes habit. In fact, research shows we can actually rewire the neural pathways in our brain, overriding old habits and developing new habits. This is referred to as *neuroplasticity*. It's a fancy way of saying...

You *can* teach an old brain new tricks.

Throughout the course of this book, our stories will highlight various aspects of the reframing pressure process. With that said, it's our belief the stories we share will be your best teacher. *Why?* Quite simply, for most of us, processes aren't as memorable as stories.

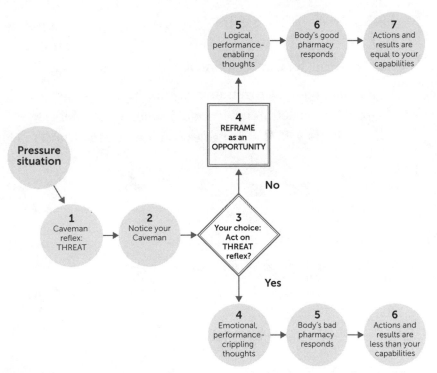

FIGURE 2.1: Two responses to pressure—act on your threat reflex or choose to reframe as an opportunity

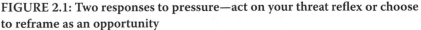

Take the high road as often as possible. It rarely has bumper to bumper traffic.

—*Author Unknown*

Highlights

- Our brains are incredibly powerful, but their reflexive reactions don't serve us well in most modern-day pressure situations.

- Our reflexive, Caveman response is to view pressure as a threat, not as an opportunity.

- Don't be hijacked by your Caveman. While we can't get rid of our Caveman, we can be aware of it and learn to manage it.

- Learn and practice the reframing skill to move from threat to opportunity. Reframing is about changing your perspective deliberately. Reframing gives you the steering wheel to your brain.

    1. Pause and recognize your Caveman's story.

    2. Challenge your Caveman's story.

    3. Explore different, rational stories.

    4. Choose and act on your best new story.

Try This

- Using the high-pressure situation you identified in Chapter 1, walk through and capture notes regarding the first two steps of the reframing process.

  - Pause and recognize your Caveman's story. *Do I want to think or feel this way?*

  - Challenge your Caveman's story. *Is this fact, fiction, or the opinion of others?*

In the following chapters, Rick and I share the songs on our crunch time playlist. Each of these songs coaches you on how to reframe from a specific threat to a specific opportunity.

3

Reframing from Trying Harder to Trying Easier

You don't get paid by the hour. You get paid by the pitch; the fewer, the better.

—*RICK PETERSON*

From the time we were young, we've learned from parents and coaches, *"It's not enough to give 100 percent; you need to give 110 percent!"* As a result, when we find ourselves stuck in a pressure-packed situation, many of us believe the best way out is to try harder.

Don't Listen to Your Parents (at least on this one)

Despite what we've been taught, at crunch time trying harder rarely works. Many examples, across a number of fields—athletic, military, and business—show that trying harder under pressure is counterproductive. Think about your best performances. Were you grinding and full of anxiety? I'm guessing no. More than likely, you remember your best performances as being almost effortless. These performances are often described as being "in the zone."

Instead of trying harder when you're under pressure, a better approach to getting in the zone is to "Try Easy!"[1]

Why Do We Try Harder Under Pressure?

We often try harder under pressure because we have some performance-limiting beliefs. For example:

- We think trying harder always produces better results.

- We think "My best is not good enough. I need to do more."

But we're wrong on both points!

In short, these beliefs cause us to view pressure situations as threatening. It's time to reframe these beliefs. As we mentioned in the previous chapter, the first step in reframing is to pause and recognize your Caveman's reflexive reactions and beliefs that cause you to think, feel, and act in ways that aren't helping you. The second step in reframing is to challenge these beliefs.

Does Trying Harder Always Produce Better Results?

We believe trying harder always produces better results. In other words, we believe there is a direct relationship between effort and performance. That relationship is shown in Figure 3.1.

When this is your belief and your performance is less than you desire, the logical solution is to try harder. As someone who has made as well as witnessed numerous six-figure and seven-figure sales presentations, I can attest to the fact that trying too hard rarely produces the results you're looking for. On the contrary, when you tell yourself things like, *"I need this sale," "I must be better than I've ever been,"* and *"I'm going to try something new to blow their socks off,"* you try harder, put more pressure on yourself,

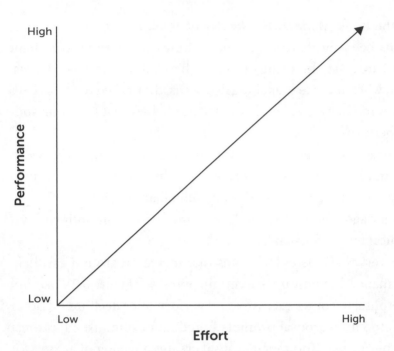

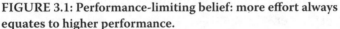

FIGURE 3.1: Performance-limiting belief: more effort always equates to higher performance.

and often reek of desperation. People don't buy from people who appear desperate.

While our culture may scream at you to try harder when you find yourself in a tough spot, the data on human performance simply doesn't support this belief. In fact, the data shows throttling back a little bit often results in better performance.

Speaking of data, Rick and the other coaches and management of the Oakland A's teams of the early 2000s borrowed a mantra from renowned statistician and management scientist W. Edwards Deming:

In God we trust. All others must bring data.

In the book *Moneyball: The Art of Winning an Unfair Game,* Michael Lewis brilliantly documents how Oakland's management refused to trust their gut or accept baseball's long-held beliefs. Rather, when it came to making decisions, they relied on data. Let's do the same as we challenge some of our beliefs that limit our ability to perform our best.

Consider a different belief that rethinks the relationship between effort and performance. Let's start with the conclusion from psychologists Robert Yerkes and John Dillingham Dodson more than a century ago. Yerkes and Dodson found there is an optimal level of arousal for performance.

The Yerkes–Dodson law states that increased arousal can help performance, but only up to a certain point (see Figure 3.2). Beyond that, arousal becomes excessive and performance declines. In other words, too little arousal prompts boredom or diminished interest in the performer. Too much arousal creates a feeling of anxiety or threat in the performer.

> ### Maximum arousal limits our performance.
>
> ### Optimal performance comes from optimal arousal.

Consider what happens when you're asked to take an exam. It's helpful to have some level of arousal to help you focus on the exam and remember the information you studied. However, when arousal goes too high, it turns into anxiety. This form of a threat impairs your ability to concentrate and makes it more difficult to remember the correct answers.

It's worth noting that those who have conducted follow-up research on the Yerkes–Dodson law have found that the optimal

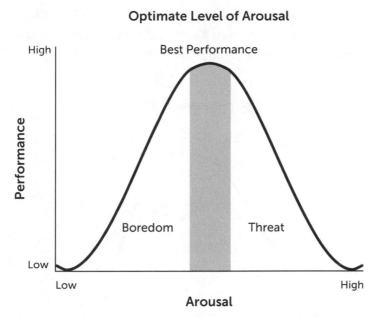

FIGURE 3.2: The Yerkes–Dodson law: the relationship between arousal and performance

level of arousal varies by task. When the task is a more complex cognitive task (e.g., making a presentation to secure funding), optimal performance results from lower levels of arousal. When the task doesn't require as much thinking (e.g., rushing the quarterback in football), optimal performance results from higher levels of arousal. Optimal arousal level also varies by person.

So now that we understand more about the relationship between arousal and performance, what's the relationship between arousal and effort? The answer to this question will give us insight into the relationship between effort and performance.

Our effort level is often directly correlated with our arousal level. When we try harder and give more effort, our arousal increases. Then it stands to reason that, just as Yerkes–Dodson shows how anxiety increases and performance declines past a certain level of arousal, our performance declines past a certain level of effort. As a result, in Figure 3.3, we can see a graph similar to the shape of Yerkes–Dodson if we replace arousal with effort.

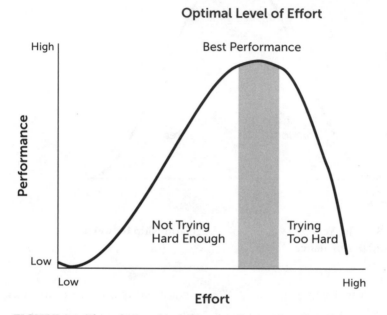

FIGURE 3.3: The relationship between effort and performance

There is a huge gap between trying your best and doing your best.

Is Nike's slogan "Just Try It!"? No, it's "Just Do It!"

—Rick Peterson

Maximum effort can cripple our performance.

Optimal performance comes from optimal effort.

So now that you know about this relationship between arousal, effort, and performance, this should raise a question for you when your performance is less than what you're capable of. Which side of the curve are you on? Are you on the left where you have low arousal and are not trying hard enough? If yes, some additional effort will improve your performance. However, when you're under pressure, more than likely your arousal and effort are too high, causing your performance to suffer. When this is the case, the answer is to Try Easy!

What Try Easy Is Not

It's worth highlighting that Try Easy is not about not trying. It's not about being lazy. It is about throttling back just a little. It's about taking the tension out of what you're doing and replacing it with a level of effort that allows you to perform in a relaxed state.

Let's look at some stories to illustrate how throttling back a bit on effort and using the Try Easy approach improves performance.

Take the Grunt Out

Sandy Koufax is arguably the greatest left-handed pitcher in baseball history. But his career didn't start out that way. After his first six years in the major leagues with the Brooklyn Dodgers, Koufax had a rather unimpressive career record of 36 wins and 40 losses. Not exactly Hall of Fame numbers. While he could throw a blazing fastball, he couldn't control it.

Koufax shared with Tom Verducci of *Sports Illustrated* the lesson that saved his career and transformed him into a Hall of Famer.[2] In 1961, Koufax was scheduled to pitch the first five innings in a Dodgers "B team" spring training game. The other pitcher who was scheduled to pitch the remainder of the game missed the flight. Koufax volunteered to pitch more innings.

Koufax's catcher and roommate on the road, Norm Sherry, urged him to ease up slightly on his fastball. Sherry thought this would improve Koufax's control and protect his arm from a potential early-season injury. Koufax took Sherry's advice and threw a no-hitter.

During this game, Koufax learned a fastball will behave better, with just as much life and better control, if you throttle back a little. As Koufax wrote in his autobiography, "I came home a different pitcher from the one who had left."[3]

That's quite the understatement from the always humble Koufax. From 1961 through his last season in 1966, Koufax amassed 129 wins against just 47 losses, winning a dominant 73 percent of his games. During these six years, he was named to the All-Star team six times and won the Cy Young Award as the league's best pitcher three times. He also won the league's Most Valuable Player (MVP) award once and finished second in the MVP voting twice. This is unheard of for a pitcher. To this day, Koufax's run of six years is considered to be one of the most dominant stretches for a pitcher in baseball history.

As a favor to Mets' owner Fred Wilpon, his former high school teammate, Koufax shared his wisdom with Rick and the Mets' pitchers during the 2004 spring training. Rick spoke with Koufax for over an hour, soaking in the teaching like a sponge. Among the lessons Koufax shared that Rick will never forget is this:

Take the grunt out. See how easy you can throw hard.

The Accidental World Record

On August 3, 2015, American swimming prodigy Katie Ledecky broke her own world record in the 1500-meter freestyle. The 18-year-old accomplished this feat during a preliminary heat at the World Championship in Kazan, Russia. The amazing thing about this world record is Ledecky wasn't trying to get it. Rather, she just happened to break a world record. Her approach? Try Easy!

Because it was a preliminary heat and not the finals, Ledecky completely detached from the outcome. She eased back on her effort and focused on swimming smoothly to preserve some of her energy for the finals.

"My coach told me to swim the first 900 meters easy, build over the next 300, then the final 300 was my choice. And to be honest, it felt pretty easy...I am pretty shocked I was able to do that. I was barely even focusing on this morning's swim. I was just so relaxed," Ledecky shared after the race.

Right after she finished, looked up at the scoreboard, and saw her time, Ledecky smiled, glanced at her coach, and gave a little shrug as if to say she was just as surprised as anyone she had broken the world record. Try Easy!

Try Easy Applied to Filmmaking[4]

The experience of my job can be like standing in the exhaust of a jet engine. I find the best way for me to deal with that is to stay calm and to emanate a sense of calm that permeates the work environment.

I think you'd find we work quietly but efficiently.

—*Steven Soderbergh*

Rick met highly decorated, world-renowned director Steven Soderbergh as Steven prepared to direct the movie *Moneyball*. The two hit it off immediately because of their shared love of baseball.

But they shared more than that. "We both love thinking about thinking," Steven told me. Despite Sony Pictures' decision to go forward with a different director for *Moneyball*, Rick and Steven have remained friends.

During my research for this book, my most interesting conversation, bar none, was with Steven. For all of his accomplishments, I found him incredibly humble and fascinating at the same time. While an entire book could be written from what he shared during our 90-minute conversation, I'm going to focus on what he shared with me regarding how Try Easy applies to filmmaking.

> I have, arguably, one of the best jobs in the world. It's a fascinating three-dimensional game in a way, in which you're dealing with large amounts of money, a significant number of people with very complex personalities, and external forces you cannot control, like weather. For some people, it can be exhilarating. I've also seen it literally just crush people and break them. It's a very pressurized situation and, if you don't respond well to pressure, it's probably not a good job.

> The last place I'm "trying hard" is on the set, in that moment, when we're trying to figure out how to do what we're doing. At that moment, I'm trying to be in the most peaceful place I can be, so I can see clearly what's really happening and what really needs to be done. And that means, in my headspace, utter and complete calm. If something's not happening, I'll slow it all down. I'll send everybody away. Because I know once the problem is solved, everything's going to go very, very quickly. It's actually more efficient to send people away, while I have a moment to step back and think about it, than to grind away on an idea or an approach I know sucks.

It's not about working harder; it's about working smarter. One of the reasons I've been able to work on as many projects as I have is because my process has improved. My creative decision-making process has become more efficient as I've done more work. This is the way it should be, but it's not always the case. Many filmmakers' trajectories are going in the opposite direction. The older they get, the longer they take to begin filming, the more the films cost, and the longer they take to shoot. They're trying harder and their results aren't as good.

My approach to life and filmmaking that has enabled me to work smarter and Try Easy boils down to three big things. First, repeat business—meaning your interactions with people should be of a quality that makes them want to continue to interact with you because, at some point, your livelihood may be continuing only because people enjoy working with you. Second, manage expectations—both your own and other people's. This is where, if expectations aren't managed effectively, conflicts happen very easily and there is an erosion of trust. When this happens, everything slows down and gets harder.

Third, and perhaps most critical, is error correction. Failure is inevitable. Sometimes things don't work. And sometimes there is such a thing as a mistake. How you handle mistakes is another crucial component to successfully navigating the world both in your life and in your work. It is fine to make a mistake; just don't keep making the same ones. By focusing on these three things, I'm much more efficient and effective than I've ever been.

The performance-limiting belief—trying harder always produces better results—is caused by a lack of knowledge. In contrast, the root cause of the next performance-limiting belief is fear.

Challenging the Fear "My Best Is Not Good Enough"

All of us have a desire to prove ourselves worthy. Most of us run into pressure situations where we fear our best won't be good enough to succeed. When we don't trust that our best performance is good enough, we try to do too much. We press.

Often, we try to do something extraordinary. We try to rise to the occasion in a few different ways:

- We give more effort.
- We try to do something we've never done before.
- We try to be perfect and avoid all mistakes.

Why aren't these good strategies?

As we learned earlier in this chapter, increasing our effort beyond a certain point actually hurts our performance.

When we try to do something we've never done before, the odds are stacked against us. It's highly unlikely that using a new approach in a high-pressure situation will produce better results than the approach we've practiced many times. There is a learning curve you cannot bypass in the heat of a pressure situation.

In addition, when we're under pressure and try to do something we've never done before, we have less control over the process. As a result, we experience an increase in fear, worry, and doubt. This deadly trio of demotivators is based on lack of knowledge, lack of skill, lack of insight, or lack of preparation. As you'd expect, when we are filled with fear, worry, and doubt, our performance suffers. Then, when we don't perform well, our confidence suffers. When our confidence suffers, our performance declines further. A vicious cycle ensues where both our confidence and our performance spiral in the wrong direction.

Furthermore, when we think our best will not be good enough, we try to be perfect and avoid all mistakes. When we do this, we perform defensively and end up making even more mistakes.

The best you're going to do is your best. You can't magically do better than you have before. Let go of the myth that in order to be successful, you need to perform better than your best under pressure. You don't.

Be Extraordinary by Being Ordinary

Rick's 2001 Oakland A's pitching staff had the second best earned run average (ERA) out of 14 teams in the American League. As the A's entered the playoffs versus the New York Yankees, Rick told his pitchers they would be extraordinary simply by being ordinary. He advised them to avoid trying to do too much. By following the same approach they had used all regular season, they would achieve the same great results, albeit on a larger stage.

Rick challenged the assumption that the playoffs required his pitchers to perform better than they did during the regular season. He reduced pressure by reminding them that they were one of the best staffs in baseball and all they needed to do in the playoffs was pitch the same way they had pitched during the regular season. Try Easy!

I Don't Need to Be Better than I Already Am

I was recently speaking with one of my friends, Mark Levy.[5] Mark is a bestselling author, positioning expert, and collaborator on ideas within this book. He shared a great story with me about a client of his, Steve Cohen. Steve is the "Millionaires' Magician" and performs his *Chamber Magic* show regularly in a suite at the Waldorf Astoria in Manhattan. He also regularly performs at the homes and events of wealthy individuals, with notable hosts including Warren Buffett, Michael Bloomberg, Martha Stewart, Michael Eisner, the Queen of Morocco, and the Crown Prince of Saudi Arabia.[6] In other words, he's used to performing under pressure.

In the spring of 2013, Steve was invited to perform on the *Late Show with David Letterman*. Mark and Steve strategized about what tricks to perform in the 3½ minutes Steve would be on *Letterman*. About ten days before the show, Mark noticed Steve becoming increasingly nervous. Mark told me he had never seen Steve get so nervous for any of his shows, regardless of who he was performing for. Mark asked Steve, "So what's the deal? Why are you so nervous?"

Steve shared with Mark, "It's *Letterman*! Millions of people are going to be watching. It'll be on YouTube forever. I've got to be great!"

In telling the story, Mark shared this with me: "Whenever someone is nervous, I always go right to logic to try to calm them down. I don't try to be inspirational. So I asked Steve, 'Have the *Letterman* talent scouts seen you perform before?'"

Steve said yes. He followed up by saying that, over the course of the past 3 years, several Letterman producers and talent bookers had been scouting his *Chamber Magic* shows at the Waldorf.

Mark responded to Steve by asking another question: "On those nights the Letterman talent scouts saw you, did you give the best performances you've ever given? Did you do every sleight perfectly?"

Steve responded by indicating they were good shows, but nothing out of the norm. He said he just did the shows like he always does.

"So what did the talent scouts think of those shows?" Mark asked.

Steve said the scouts told him they loved his shows. They told him they wanted him to perform on *Letterman*.

Mark followed up with Steve "So *Letterman* knows what it is they are getting, right? They saw you perform a few times."

They didn't say to themselves, "Hmm, this guy is okay. Maybe if we put him on *Letterman* with millions of people watching and our reputations on the line, he's going to do better. Let's give him that chance." They didn't say that, right?

"They saw your normal show and said, 'This is the guy we want to put on the show to perform in front of millions of people.' Who you are now is exactly who they want."

Mark's advice—you don't need to be better than you are—helped soothe Steve's anxiety. For the week leading up to his appearance, he was relatively relaxed. Steve's performance on *Letterman* was awesome (*www.youtube.com/watch?v=cpSAI29kCog*).

> I will be extraordinary by being ordinary.
>
> I don't need to be better than I already am.
>
> Right here, right now, I'm as good as I'm going to be.
>
> I will Try Easy!

Highlights

- Trying harder under pressure is often counterproductive; it leads to a decline in performance. More than likely, you remember your best performances as almost effortless.

- We often try harder under pressure because we have some performance-limiting beliefs that have permeated our thinking. Pause, recognize, and challenge these performance-limiting beliefs, many of which are the result of fear. Then trade these performance-limiting beliefs for performance-enhancing beliefs.

- Trying harder doesn't always produce better results. Optimal performance comes from optimal effort.

  - Think of the lesson from Koufax: take the grunt out. See how easy you can throw hard!

  - Think of Katie Ledecky and how she was completely relaxed when accomplishing her accidental world record.

- Right here, right now, I'm as good as I'm going to be. I don't need to be better than I already am.

  - Think of Rick's message to the Oakland A's in the 2001 playoffs: Be extraordinary by being ordinary!

  - Think of Mark Levy's advice to magician Steve Cohen before going on *David Letterman*: "They saw your normal show and said, 'This is the guy we want to put on the show to perform in front of millions of people.'"

Try This

- Identify one specific activity where trying your hardest may be hurting your performance.

- Develop a game plan for how you can throttle back to a relaxed 90-percent effort.

- Put your game plan into practice and compare the results of your performance with the two methods.

- Adjust your effort as needed to reach optimal performance.

4

Reframing from Tension to Laughter

Always go to other people's funerals, otherwise they won't come to yours.

—*YOGI BERRA*

A ll other things being equal, a performer who is tense loses to a performer who is relaxed. We all know we need to relax under pressure, but we don't know how. In fact, when we're told to relax and have fun, this often frustrates us and makes us even tenser. Why? Because we don't know how to relax when we're under pressure.

Let me offer up a solution. In your tensest moments, actively seek opportunities to laugh. There is something about laughter that makes threats less daunting and opportunities more visible.

In this chapter, Rick and I will coach you on how to use humor as the best antidote to tension. I will also share a number of examples of Rick and others using humor to relieve tension and move forward in difficult situations. Humor is more than a nice-to-have; it's a must-have. Not just because it's fun, but because it works.

How Does Humor Work in Pressure Situations?

Andrew Tarvin is the chief humorist at the company he founded, Humor That Works. He is not what pops into my head when I think of a humorist. For one, he is not a comedian. He graduated with a degree in computer science and engineering from The Ohio State University. Before founding Humor That Works, Andrew worked as a successful international information technology (IT) project manager at Procter & Gamble. He said, "As an engineer, I find what works, I do it, and then I teach it to other people. It turns out humor works."[1] But how does it work?

Psychologically

These are just some of the many psychological benefits of humor:

- Without humor, we tend to exaggerate the importance of pressure situations. Humor helps us put things into perspective and see situations as less daunting.

- Humor helps us laugh at ourselves, lowers our defense mechanisms, and opens us up to receive instruction or feedback.

- Humor helps improve information recall and increases long-term retention.[2]

- Having a good laugh is incompatible with anxiety and fear.[3]

- Humor strengthens relationships. It's a way for people to show support for each other. When you laugh with someone, you're standing on the same side.[4]

- Humor improves creativity and problem solving.[5]

Physiologically

The old adage "laughter is the best medicine" is confirmed by medical research. When you start to laugh, it doesn't just lighten your load mentally. It actually induces physical, performance-enhancing changes in your body.[6]

- Laughter stops the body's stress response in its tracks. It relaxes muscles and decreases blood pressure. The muscle relaxation that comes after laughing has subsided can last for up to 45 minutes.[7]

- Laughter increases the release of endorphins, brain chemicals which reduce physical and psychological pain and boost immunity.

- Laughter increases your intake of oxygen-rich air and stimulates your heart, lungs, and muscles.

Additional Benefits

In addition to helping our minds and bodies, humor in the workplace has been shown to reduce absenteeism, increase company loyalty, prevent burnout, and increase productivity.[8]

In a study published in a 2012 issue of *Humor: International Journal of Humor Research*, Thomas Ford and colleagues at Western Carolina University tested the effects of humor on anxiety and math performance. The researchers gathered participants and purposefully stressed them out by telling them they would be taking a difficult math test as part of the experiment. Then the participants were separated into three groups.

- Group A participants read humorous comic books.

- Group B participants read poems.

- Group C participants read nothing at all.

Compared to Group B and C participants, the Group A participants exposed to humor not only reported less anxiety about the test, they also scored significantly better.[9]

Furthermore, if you're not yet convinced of the benefits of laughter, let's speak to your wallet. One study found both executives' performance ratings and bonuses were positively correlated with their use of humor.[10]

> Humor isn't just a fun, nice-to-have tool in pressure situations; it's a must-have weapon in your arsenal.

Why Don't More People Use Humor in Tense Situations?

The predominant force that stifles humor in adults is the fear of appearing foolish or silly.[11] In the workplace, people fear being labeled unprofessional.

The reality is many adults actively seek out others who make them laugh. This is true even in the workplace. In a study of over 700 CEOs, 98 percent of them preferred job candidates with a sense of humor.[12] Furthermore, leaders who use humor are viewed as being on top of things, being in charge and in control. This is true even when the leaders don't feel they are in control.

When it comes to your fear of appearing foolish or unprofessional, recognize this is your Caveman talking to you. Challenge your Caveman. Remember, the facts show people favor those with a sense of humor.

Break Out the Sharpies![13]

As I was writing this chapter, I knew I wanted to include a work-related example or two showing how others use humor to relieve tension. I reached out to Mac Delaney, a great friend, who is one of the funniest people I know. Mac is also an executive and thought leader in digital advertising.

To add to his résumé, Mac is also the poster boy of someone who has reframed his work life from tension to laughter. At age 26, Mac was taking the same dose of blood pressure medication as a 70-year-old. A little more than a decade later, he remains committed to excellence in his work, but he does so through a lens that relies on humor to relieve tension and achieve results. He also happens to be free of the need for any blood pressure medication.

I felt confident Mac would have many examples to share of how he uses humor to depressurize tense work situations. He didn't disappoint. Here is just one of many examples he shared with me.

> In 2013, when I was at VivaKi, our team was going through a rough patch. The general manager in our New York office had left. Many team members followed the GM out, which made everyone's job harder because each person remaining was now doing the work of two people. In addition, the holiday season fast approached, a time when the ad world is filled with twice the volume of work, creating extraordinary tension and pressure.
>
> I told our leadership team I was going to make weekly visits from Chicago to New York from October through the end of the year. This was an attempt to stabilize and keep our New York team—the largest of our teams—from being crushed by the pressure. We were going to lock arms and get through the year together.
>
> During one of my trips, I noticed Banksy—a famous graffiti artist whose art contains social messages—was in town for a one-month show. This gave me an idea. I went down to a convenience store and bought a bunch of big Sharpies (permanent magic markers). Our New York office in SoHo was brand new. While the location was great, the walls had not yet been

painted, so they were all white. The office was awful—totally sterile. Picture the scene out of the movie *Office Space*. We had been told for a while the walls were going to be painted in our company colors, but it hadn't happened yet.

I came into the office one day before anyone arrived. Doing my best Banksy impression, I wrote all over the walls with my Sharpie. I wrote messages like, "Who better than us?" and "It's our time!" and added data points showing the impressive volume we had done that year.

When everyone arrived at the office, they were shocked. Our head of HR was not happy. Our CEO loved it. Then I handed out the remaining Sharpies to the team members and said, "We're all going to do our own Banksy." Everybody on the team jumped on board at the opportunity. It was a huge release for the team that countered all of the negative stress that had been coming at us. It took on a life of its own. For the first time in a long time, people were smiling and laughing.

It provided us with some much-needed perspective that had been lost amidst the tension. We regularly reminded each other, "We are not performing brain surgery; we are selling ads on the Internet." It doesn't mean you care less. In fact, your work gets better when you see the world through that lens of humor. It's a core value we can't give up, especially in the creative world. Humor and creativity go hand in hand.

Finding Humor, Even in Dark Places

Throughout the interviews I conducted with athletes, soldiers, and business leaders, I found it interesting the number of times they used humor to cope with tense situations and relieve pressure. Humor is your Caveman's kryptonite.

While it's hard to imagine a spirit of fun and playfulness emerging in stress-filled war zones where people's survival is at stake, there are many well-documented examples of using humor to cope during war. In World War II, for example, Londoners joked more than usual during Nazi bombing attacks. When Winston Churchill was told Mussolini had decided to enter the war in 1939, he announced to the British people,

> *The Italians have announced they will fight on the Nazis' side.*
>
> *I think it's only fair. We had to put up with them last time.*

The doctors and support staff in the 1970s TV series *M*A*S*H*— one of the highest-rated shows in U.S. television history—exemplified the importance of humor in the face of extraordinary stress and pressure. The show revolved around key personnel in the U.S. Army's 4077th Mobile Army Surgical Hospital (MASH) unit in the Korean War. In the face of horrific tragedy, injury, and death, the humor exchanged among the show's characters sometimes seemed inappropriate, even downright mean-spirited. The point, however, was the power of humor to keep the characters sane, competent, and effective under these immense wartime pressures. By helping the members of the medical team to remain clear headed, their humor literally saved lives.

Humor momentarily reduces the perceived threat posed by the situation. It also helps generate a

dark comedy
[dahrk kom-i-dee]
Humor that makes light of subject matter usually considered taboo

sense of control and provides perspective that helps you see dire situations with some level of amusement.

A keen sense of humor helps us overlook the unbecoming, understand the unconventional, tolerate the unpleasant, overcome the unexpected, and outlast the unbearable.

—*Billy Graham*

Humor can be found in the worst of circumstances.

If others have found humor in the midst of war,
I can and will find humor in my pressure situations.

While a major league baseball clubhouse is far from a war zone, players and coaches also find comfort in dark humor to cope with difficult circumstances. Jim Abbott shared one example of this during an interaction with Rick.

They'll Entomb You in the Hall of Fame

Jim is a highly decorated pitcher. In 1987, while at the University of Michigan, Jim won the James E. Sullivan Award as the nation's best amateur athlete. In 1988, Jim was voted Big Ten Athlete of the Year. At the 1988 Summer Olympics, he pitched the U.S. to victory versus Cuba in the gold-medal-winning game. As a starting pitcher with the New York Yankees, Jim threw a no-hitter.

For those of you who haven't heard Jim's story, you'll be amazed to learn he accomplished all of this despite having been born without a right hand. From a young age, he learned to throw the ball left-handed and then quickly transfer his baseball glove from the stub on his right arm to his left hand so he could field any balls hit back to him.

In 1991, his third year in the major leagues, Jim had an outstanding year with the California Angels, with 18 wins, 11 losses, and a 2.89 earned run average (ERA). In the four seasons that followed, at best Jim was average. He had 38 wins and 45 losses and wasn't pitching up to his standards. Heading into the 1995 season, Jim desperately wanted to pitch well again. He was a free agent and joined the Chicago White Sox, where Rick served as the bullpen coach and pitching coach for the relievers.

In Jim's first spring training outing of 1995, he failed to get a single batter out before being pulled from the game. He was devastated and felt threatened. Reflexively, Jim's Caveman started flooding his mind with crippling thoughts. *Is my spot on the team in jeopardy? What do my teammates and coaches think of me?* Keenly aware of this, Rick left a note on Jim's locker. "Sometimes you need to take a couple steps back to take a running leap."

"Even though the game hadn't gone the way I wanted it to, Rick's note made me feel as though I had people in my corner on this new team. It said a lot about the way Rick approached things. It built trust between us that served as a foundation for later conversations," Jim shared with me.

At one point during spring training, Rick watched Jim throw a practice session in the bullpen. Rick said it appeared Jim was rushing to get his glove onto his throwing hand before finishing his pitching motion. It appeared he was scared about being able to defend himself against a line drive hit right back at him. Rick remembered Jim had been hit by a line drive the previous year.

When Jim was with the Yankees, he'd had thrown a fastball to Frank Thomas, one of the best line drive hitters in the league. "I threw a pitch and Frank Thomas hit a line drive back at me. Bang-bang, it hit me in my left leg really hard. When Thomas returned to the dugout, he told teammates he'd never hit a ball harder. The next day the bruise started at my thigh and ended at my ankle. It healed pretty quickly and I didn't think about it too much.

"I'd never really thought about defending myself on the mound. That was for other people to worry about. The ball Thomas hit, had it been a couple feet higher, might have killed me. But, if I was shortening my delivery as a result, going for the glove too soon and cutting off my momentum to the plate, it was subconscious. It was instinct. It was survival."[14] The Caveman effect.

Rick continued his conversation with Jim, "Do you know how many guys have ever died on a baseball field?" Before Jim could answer, Rick answered his own question, "None!"

"So why don't you just finish the pitch? If you don't, the pitch is not going to be effective and someone's probably going to hit a line drive off your face. And if that happens to you, you'll go right to the Hall of Fame. They'll take your uniform right off and ship it to the Hall of Fame. They'll entomb you in the Hall of Fame."

"It was dark humor that is typical in a sports locker room, but Rick was right," Jim shared. "He got me to see I had to let go of my fear of being hit and finish my pitch. In his own unique way, he helped me realize that, even though I would be left defenseless, I would be less likely to get hit if I completed my follow-through and made a better pitch. If I did get hit, I'd be wheeled away to the Hall of Fame. It was kind of twisted, but I laughed and it helped me realize I needed to do something different."

By late July, Jim had six wins and four losses. His ERA was 3.36, more than a run better than the season before. From the end of May through the middle of summer, his ERA was under 3. Jim shared, "With Rick's help, I could be aggressive, and it was exhilarating. I'd wondered if I would ever be that guy again, and now I was."

As you know, humor comes in many forms. Although this section focused on the use of dark humor to relieve tension in difficult circumstances, the reality is any humor that amuses you or allows you to smile produces the same performance-enhancing effect.

What If I'm Not Funny?

Just like the person who is told to relax, you may feel tense when being told to be funny. Easier said than done, right? Here's the good news. Just as you don't need to be a gourmet chef to enjoy food, you don't need to be a comedian to enjoy humor. You can consume the humor created by others.

What type of humor works best? Like beauty, humor is in the eyes, ears, and mind of the beholder. Think about what amuses you, makes you smile, or makes you laugh. It could be anyone or anything—your kids, your crazy dog, a friend, a TV show, a movie scene, standup comedy, a YouTube video, a book, a song, an image, or maybe even your golf game.

With the availability of so many great sources of humor, you should never be left wanting. However, if you're on your own, your iPhone has run out of battery, and you can't picture something in your mind, do what Rick does, what Jerry Seinfeld does, and what so many other funny people do. Observe life. Take in your surroundings and look for people or things that amuse you. Recognize the funny things people say and do. Comment on those things. Sometimes just the laugh or the smile itself is enough to trigger the performance-enhancing response.

Highlights

- Humor has been proven to provide numerous benefits, including healthier minds and bodies. Humor in the workplace has been shown to reduce absenteeism, increase company loyalty, prevent burnout, and increase productivity. When it comes to pressure situations, humor is a must-have weapon in your arsenal.

- Humor can often be found in dark places. It momentarily reduces the perceived threat posed by the situation. It also helps generate a sense of control and provides perspective that can help you see dire situations with some levity.

- Think of Mac Delaney and his team breaking out the Sharpies and doing their best Banksy impersonations on the sterile office walls. This humorous activity provided them with some much-needed perspective that had been lost amidst the tension.

- Think of Rick's message to cut through Jim Abbott's struggles and fear with humor: Just finish the pitch. If you don't, you'll get hit in the face and they'll wheel you away and entomb you in the Hall of Fame.

- Just as you don't need to be a gourmet chef to enjoy food, you don't need to be funny to enjoy humor.

Try This

- Think about what amuses you, makes you smile, or makes you laugh. It could be anyone or anything.

- For your sources of humor that are recorded or available online, gather these into an easily accessible place (e.g., your smart phone).

- Tap into your sources of humor the next time you're getting ready for a big performance. Reap the performance-enhancing benefits of your laughter.

5

Reframing from Anxiety to Taking Control

You are a professional glove hitter. Hit the glove!

—*RICK PETERSON*

There are many things about pressure situations which cause our anxiety levels to rise. The reasons include, but aren't limited to, these:

- We focus on goals or factors outside of our control.
- We focus on outcomes rather than the process to achieve those outcomes.
- We get overwhelmed by the perceived difficulty of the task.
- We commit to doing too much.
- Our expectations are too high because we use the wrong measuring stick.
- We exaggerate the importance of the situation.

In this chapter, we share a number of antidotes to pressure that will lower your anxiety levels and put you back in control.

Hitting the Glove

At the beginning of spring training every year, Rick asks his pitchers, "What's your goal?" Most of the answers given center around outcomes like winning a certain number of games, or pitching a certain number of innings. Rick takes these answers as an opportunity to teach a lesson in goal setting. While many of us have been taught to set lofty, long-term-outcome goals, the type that show up on the back of a baseball card or a company financial statement, these goals are overrated in comparison to lesser-appreciated, short-term, bite-sized process goals.

What's wrong with focusing on lofty outcome goals? It can lead to unhealthy distractions, such as focusing on factors outside your control. For example, winning a baseball game has many factors outside the pitcher's control—how many runs his team scores, how well his team fields, how well the opposing hitters handle good pitches, and even the calls of the umpire.

In addition, the magnitude of a lofty outcome goal that was initially inspiring and motivating can become intimidating and demoralizing, causing doubt and anxiety that hurts performance.

Rick refocuses his pitchers on simple, short-term, bite-sized process goals. He tells them they are professional glove hitters. Their goal is, quite simply, to hit the catcher's glove as often as possible with the right pitch.

"Hit the glove!" is the mantra Rick uses to tame his pitchers' Caveman thinking and keep them focused on what they can control. By focusing on this simple process goal, they are able to avoid being distracted by things outside their control.

At times, it can get overwhelming. You're thinking, "Oh man. I've got to face these four hitters and they're all really good hitters and I've got runners on 2nd and 3rd base. What do I do? How am

I going to get out of this?" Rick would really simplify it to where you felt really comfortable. At the end of the day, all you had to do was go out there and throw the ball into the catcher's glove and then let the rest take care of itself.[1]

—*Chad Bradford, Oakland A's reliever featured prominently in* Moneyball

---

In addition to increasing focus, hitting the glove on a high percentage of pitches is also the most probable path to achieving larger, outcome-oriented individual and team goals.

Greg Maddux's Unorthodox Performance Appraisal

Starting pitcher Greg Maddux was asked after a game to assess his performance. His assessment surprised people. He didn't talk about whether he got the win, how the other team hit him, or even the number of runs they scored. Instead, Maddux's succinct answer was "73 out of 78." Reporters didn't understand.

What Maddux meant was that he threw 73 out of his 78 pitches the way he intended. This was a good day in his estimation. Everything that happened to the ball after it left his fingers was beyond his control.[2]

This mental discipline of focusing on only what he could control served him well. Maddux won more games in the 1990s than any other pitcher. He is the only pitcher in Major League history to win at least 15 games for 17 straight seasons. He is the first pitcher in Major League history to win the Cy Young Award, given to the league's best pitcher, for four consecutive years (1992–1995). In 2014, Maddux was voted into the Baseball Hall of Fame in his first year of eligibility, receiving more votes than any other player.

Chunking: Can You Focus for Three Seconds at a Time?

When we feel like the task we need to perform under pressure is more difficult than we can handle, we are filled with fear and anxiety and feel threatened. An effective strategy for reducing the perceived difficulty and corresponding threat is chunking.

Chunking refers to the process of breaking down a seemingly overwhelming goal into smaller, bite-sized pieces. In other words, don't try to eat the elephant in one bite. Rather, eat the elephant one bite at a time. By breaking down large goals into realistically achievable steps, chunking reduces anxiety and increases feelings of confidence and control. It helps us flip the switch from Caveman to Conscious Thinker.

By creating a series of simple, short-term, bite-sized process goals linked to a larger outcome goal, you get to recognize success more frequently. Every time a goal is achieved, your body releases dopamine, the feel-good neurotransmitter. The resulting dopamine makes you feel confident and productive.

We all know focus is required to perform at a high level. Yet, when we cannot keep our focus for an extended period of time, it's easy to get anxious and feel like we're not up to the challenge. Clutch performers don't focus for longer periods of time. Rather, they focus at the right times. They have specific entry and exit points that allow them to focus intensely when needed.

In 1994, Rick was promoted from the Chicago White Sox AAA affiliate in Nashville to the big league team. Rick was both the bullpen coach as well as a codirector of the White Sox sports psychology program. He was asked by Ron Schueler and Jackie Brown, the White Sox general manager and pitching coach respectively, to try his hand with Roberto Hernandez, a relief pitcher who was struggling. Bert, as Hernandez was known by his coaches and teammates, had blown a number of recent save opportunities and his confidence had plummeted. In the prior season, Bert performed excellently. He saved 39 games, including four scoreless innings and a save in the American League Championship Series.

Rick hadn't seen anything wrong with the mechanics of Bert's pitching motion. He asked Bert a number of questions to try to diagnose the cause of Bert's struggles. Based on Bert's answers, Rick thought Bert might be losing focus and giving in to distractions while he was on the mound.

During a bullpen practice session, Rick asked Bert, "What is your pre-pitch routine? What do you say to yourself to mentally lock in a pitch?"

Bert responded, "After I get the sign from the catcher, I tell myself, 'Let it go and make your pitch!'"

Rick said, "Okay, so that locks the pitch in for you. So let's do it. Say it out loud and then make your pitch."

As Bert started his pre-pitch routine, Rick timed him with a stopwatch. From the time Bert got the sign from the catcher, voiced his mental instructions, and released the ball from his fingertips, it took 3 seconds.

Rick asked Bert, "Can you focus for 3 seconds at a time?" Bert confirmed he could.

Rick continued, "In a typical one-inning appearance, you throw 15 pitches. That's 45 seconds of focus to get a save. So to save 40 games, and have a great season, you need to focus intensely for 1,800 seconds or 30 minutes this season. You'll focus better by focusing less. Can you do that?"

Bert calmed down. He chuckled at how simple it sounded.

Rick's reframe, "focus better by focusing less," and his ability to break down a larger, lofty outcome goal (40 saves for the season) into a goal for each pitch (focus for 3 seconds and hit the glove) helped Bert move from anxious to confident and in control, from threat to opportunity, from Caveman to Conscious Thinker.

> To relieve pressure, ditch lofty outcome goals.
>
> Focus on simple, short-term, bite-sized process goals.

Hitting the Glove and Chunking Applied to My Career

I've worked in sales for many years. The beginning of each year is one of the moments when salespeople's anxiety levels are at their highest. The number you produced last year is a thing of the past. The scoreboard is turned back to zero. Your new and enlarged multimillion-dollar quota is staring you right in the face. You have to prove yourself all over again, and again, and again.

In many sales organizations, it's viewed as motivational to talk about hitting big numbers—to talk about how much more you're going to deliver this year compared to last. Despite positive intentions, the rally cry of "We're raising the bar!" leads some to shed tears. While this is intended to be motivational, the result is often fear, worry, and doubt.

Why? Because, just like pitchers, as salespeople, we know there are many parts of the sales game that are beyond our control. Also, it's easy to lose focus amidst the cornucopia of daily distractions.

After I heard Rick talk about "Hit the glove!" I immediately began to think of what my day-to-day sales version of hitting the glove was. I settled on *high-quality interactions with customers and prospects.* I defined a high-quality interaction as any interaction with the customer or prospective customer that advances a sale and/or our relationship. If I simply focused on having high-quality interactions with customers on a daily basis, I would make great progress toward putting a dent in my quota.

Once I defined my version of hitting the glove, I began to think about how many high-quality interactions I should have each day. I set the initial target at two. Before you laugh and ask what I was going to do after lunch, consider the math. If I had two high-quality interactions per day, that was 10 per week. That was 40 per month. Assuming one month of vacation, that was 440 per year. That was many more than I had been averaging.

As soon as I started focusing on my new simple, short-term, bite-sized process goal of two high-quality interactions with customers each day, I began thinking about my day differently. I began prioritizing the two high-quality interactions with customers above everything else. As I considered how to invest my time, I regularly asked myself, *"Is this helping me hit the glove?"*

As a result, my focus improved remarkably. I wasted less time. I didn't give my quota a second thought. My numbers took off, and I finished the year more than 25 percent ahead of my prior year's performance. Small changes, big results.

Forget about Your Personal Best. Beat Your Average![3, 4]

In many cases, the pressure we feel comes from evaluating our performance using the wrong measuring stick. By doing so, we create false expectations and increased levels of anxiety.

In some cases, we compare ourselves to others who are at the top of their game. This makes no more sense than it does for a weekend golfer to compare himself to the top professional golfer in the world. Even if we compare ourselves to others who are closer to our skill level, we often overinflate the others' strengths and ignore their weaknesses while minimizing our strengths and exaggerating our weaknesses. More often than not, comparing ourselves to others triggers our Caveman, leading to feelings of anxiety, frustration, and discouragement.

Comparison is the thief of joy.

—*Theodore Roosevelt*

A better way to evaluate your performance is to compare yourself with you. I spoke with Dr. Julie Bell about how to do it in a way that not only reduces anxiety and increases confidence, but also results in continuous performance improvement. "Dr. J," as her clients call her, is a sports psychologist for professional and amateur athletes as well as a business coach to organizations like Southwest Airlines, Microsoft, and State Farm.

Dr. J created the following personal performance evaluation scale.

Personal Performance Evaluation Scale

0 = Your Worst   5 = Your Average   10 = Your Best

FIGURE 5.1: Personal Performance Evaluation Scale

On the far left is a 0, which represents *your personal worst performance* on a chosen activity. For me, in my role as a leadership and human performance solutions advisor, assume this equates to three high-quality interactions during a given week.

On the far right is a 10, which represents *your personal best performance* on a chosen activity. For me, assume this equates to 20 high-quality interactions during a given week.

Most importantly, the 5 in the middle of the scale represents *your average. Average is where you consistently perform today.*

For me, assume this equates to 10 high-quality interactions per week.

Dr. J encourages the clients she coaches not to be distracted by the word *average*. She says, "Let's be honest. Few people want to be average." Remember, this is not an average relative to a group of people like your colleagues. It's your personal average. Identifying your personal average lets you know where you stand. Even better, it lets you know you have more game in you.

Based on this scale, Dr. J asks her clients, "How bad does a performance have to be before you consider it a failure?" Most people say anywhere below their personal average is a failure. Dr. J agrees.

The next question she asks is more telling: "How good does a performance have to be for you to consider it a success?" Many people say it has to be a 10, at least as good as their personal best.

Personal Performance Evaluation Scale

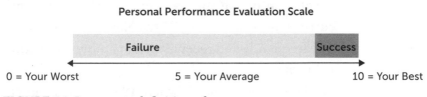

FIGURE 5.2: Inaccurate definition of success

If you don't think this type of thinking exists, it does. My daughter, Julia, is in high school and has swum competitively for the past decade. Swimmers religiously compare their times to their PB, or personal best. I can attest to the fact that regularly comparing yourself to your personal best is more harmful than helpful. It's not uncommon to see swimmers frustrated, anxious, and sometimes even shedding tears when they fail to reach a personal best.

Evaluating your success relative to your personal best is dangerous. *Why?* It's an unrealistic expectation. Only a small percentage of the time do you beat your personal best. Therefore, if you define success only as a 10, most performances are viewed as failures. Evaluating your performance as a failure on a frequent basis leads to increased anxiety and frustration, and decreased confidence.

Let's continue with my earlier example where I average 10 high-quality interactions during a week. Assume one week I have 13 high-quality interactions. If I only define 20 high-quality inter-actions as a success, then I will finish the week where I had 13 feeling as though I failed. *So what's the alternative?*

The Real Bell Curve: A Better Way of Evaluating Success and Failure

Peak performers understand the need to recognize success on a daily basis. Success builds confidence and is a powerful motivator. Rather than equating success only with the infrequent times you beat your personal best, define success as any performance that exceeds your current personal average. This allows you to recog-nize success more frequently and receive the dopamine boosts that go along with achieving goals.

Continuing with my earlier example where 10 high-quality inter-actions per week is my average, when I have 11 or more high-qual-ity interactions during a week, I should view that week as a success. Yes, I am capable of greater performance, but my evaluation for the week allows me to head into next week with less anxiety and greater levels of confidence. This increases the likelihood I will be motivated and beat my average again.

Personal Performance Evaluation Scale

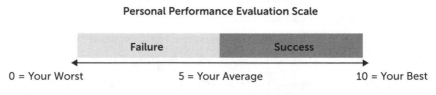

FIGURE 5.3: Accurate evaluation of success and failure

Yeah, but...

You may be saying to yourself, "This may make sense for a slacker like Judd, but it won't work for me. I'm tougher on myself than anyone else. That's what drives me to get better."

Dr. J's response: "Is evaluating your performance as a failure more often than as a success truly leading you to perform better? The answer is no. When you evaluate an above-your-personal-average performance as a failure, it is more frustrating than motivating. It's likely to leave you feeling like nothing you do is good enough. That creates anxiety and is a recipe for disaster."

It's important to highlight that evaluating an above-average performance as a success and being satisfied with that performance is not the same thing.

If I have an above-average week for me with 11 or more high-quality interactions, I recognize I have more game in me and I'm motivated to perform even better next week.

The key question to ask yourself is this: *What method of self-evaluation is likely to reduce my anxiety and drive the greatest levels of confidence and motivation next week?* Being tough on yourself and viewing any performance that doesn't reach your personal best as a failure? Or knowing your personal average and viewing any performance above that as a success?

Yeah, but Doesn't This Approach Encourage Mediocrity?

It would if your personal average stayed the same, but it doesn't. As your performance improves, your personal average shifts. What was previously above average—a 6 on the Personal Performance Evaluation Scale of 0–10—soon becomes your new 5. As you redefine your new average, you take your game to the next level. Your average is continually improving as your performance improves.

And because your average is always a 5 on a scale of 0–10, it shows you still have more game in you.

Mindfulness as a Tool to Reframing: Being Here...Now

One of the practices Rick relies on daily to cast off anxiety, tame his Caveman, keep his mind relaxed, and reframe from threat to opportunity is mindfulness. Mindfulness teaches you to pay attention to the present moment, recognize your thoughts and emotions, and keep them under control, especially when you are faced with stressful, pressure-filled situations.

Rick isn't alone. In addition to its widespread use among elite professional athletes, coaches, and teams, the use of mindful practices is taking hold at successful companies such as Google, General Mills, Goldman Sachs, Apple, Medtronic, and Aetna.[5]

While mindfulness is often associated with meditation, it includes a wide range of practices used to calm the mind and gain clarity of thought. Additional mindful practices include, but aren't limited to, prayer, journaling, and physical exercise.

> **mindfulness**
> [mahynd-fuh l-nis]
> *Paying attention in a particular way—on purpose, in the present moment, and nonjudgmentally*

"The important thing is to have a regular introspective practice that takes you away from your daily routines and enables you to reflect on your work and your life—to really focus on what is truly important to you," says Bill George, former CEO of Medtronic, author of *True North*, and teacher of Authentic Leadership at Harvard Business School.[6]

There's an entire body of science backing the idea that increased mindfulness can equate to better performance. Studies find daily meditation helps raise awareness of self-defeating thoughts. Mindfulness practice also helps reduce the production of cortisol, the fight, flight, or freeze hormone that contributes directly to anxiety and distracting mental chatter.

Michael Gervais is a high-performance sports psychologist who has been the Seattle Seahawks' team consultant since 2012. He says of the Seahawks players who are engaged in mindful practices, "They've learned to think more clearly under pressure. We can learn something here from some of the best athletes in the world. What they do can be used outside of football. It's relevant to any type of performance whether it's on the football field, [in] the board room or [in] the living room."[7]

Lelia O'Connor, an executive leadership coach and pioneer in teaching mindfulness in the workplace, says, "Through mindfulness, you become more aware of how negative thoughts and feelings impact your stress level, which limits your ability to perform at your best. You gain greater understanding of how to transform pressure situations into opportunities to act with greater freedom, ease, calm, and effectiveness. For anyone working in fast-paced, pressure-packed environments—and that's most of us—mindfulness is a performance-enhancing skill."

My Personal Application of These Antidotes to Anxiety

I've regularly used the techniques shared in this chapter—hitting the glove, chunking, beating my average, and mindfulness—as I write this book. When Rick and I first discussed writing a book together, we shared our goals for the book. We both want this book to change readers' lives for the better and also to enable readers to positively influence the lives of others. While this lofty goal is inspiring, it can also be intimidating. It can lead to expectations that are hard to live up to. It can trigger my Caveman, resulting in feelings of anxiety and fear, which can be paralyzing.

Instead of thinking about our lofty goal as I sit down to write, I take the pressure off by keeping it simple. I hit the glove and chunk a 35,000-word manuscript down to size by writing 500 to 1,000 words per day. I minimize the importance of my writing by telling myself I'm not trying to change the world; I'm sharing some of the cool things I've learned through speaking with Rick and a number of elite performers. Every day, I seek to beat my average. I recognize some of what I write will be average or worse and will never leave my laptop. Some of what I write will be better than my average and will make it into the final manuscript. If I'm ever feeling pressured to write and it's being imposed on me, I reframe by saying to myself, "I don't *have to* write. I *get to* write about a topic I'm passionate about."

Highlights

- At crunch time, uncertainty is your enemy and control is your friend. Be a control freak. Do everything you can to control those things which are under your control. Ignore everything else.

- Ditch lofty outcome goals that can be intimidating and paralyzing. Set simple, short-term, bite-sized process goals that are completely under your control. Think "Hit the glove!"

- Use chunking to reduce the perceived difficulty of the task. Think of Bert: Focus for 3 seconds per pitch (times 15 pitches per save) = 45 seconds per save (times 40 saves per season) = 1,800 seconds per season (divided by 60 seconds per minute) = 30 minutes per season.

- Change your measuring stick to one that reduces anxiety. Beat your personal average and build on the resulting confidence.

- Mindfulness practices are no longer just for Tibetan monks, elite athletes, and executives. They are for anyone working in fast-paced, pressure-filled environments.

- Instead of thinking in terms of "I *have* to...," think in terms of "I *get* to...."

Try This

- Identify a daunting, outcome-oriented goal that has you feeling under pressure.

- Figure out your version of "Hit the glove!" by chunking it down into one or more simple, short-term, bite-sized process goals. If you're still feeling intimidated, chunk it down further until you've got it to a point where the process goal seems relatively easy.

- Recognize and reward yourself for the progress you make on this process goal. Your confidence will grow and your brain will thank you with a dose of dopamine. This will help you keep your momentum.

- If you aren't already, begin practicing mindfulness—meditation, prayer, journaling, or physical exercise such as walking or yoga—to calm your mind and enable you to see pressure situations with a fresh perspective.

You've now heard the first three songs on our crunch time playlist. What are your thoughts? How are you applying this to your pressure situations? Share with us via email at *judd@juddhoekstra.com* or at *facebook.com/CrunchTimePerformance*.

6

Reframing from Doubt to Confidence

A lot of really good players I've been around believe they're a lot better than they really are. They're not constantly evaluating themselves critically. In a game like baseball, that every-day evaluation can be so detrimental. They're smart enough to forget the negatives of the past and somehow only draw from the positive. As a result, these guys end up being better than their physical talent says they should be.[1]

—BILLY BEANE, executive vice president of baseball operations, Oakland A's

Our reflexive thoughts and assumptions under pressure often lead us to feelings of fear, worry, and doubt. These reflexive thoughts and assumptions include, but aren't limited to these:

- We base our confidence on our most recent performance.
- We assume we have to feel great to perform great.
- We assume we are stuck in the present, pressure situation.
- We fail to recognize our strengths and focus on our doubts.

The elite performers I interviewed boosted their confidence in unconventional ways. In this chapter, you'll learn the methods these elite performers use to overcome their doubts and increase their confidence.

Shifting Your Source of Confidence from Unreliable to Reliable

Most people base their confidence about an upcoming performance on their most recent performance. When they perform well, they're confident. When they don't perform well, they aren't. The obvious drawback of this approach is that performance fluctuates, in some cases based on conditions outside your control.

When you let your confidence fluctuate based on your performance, you find yourself in a downward spiral of doubt. If you perform poorly, you lose confidence, which leads to another poor performance, further eroding your confidence. *What's the alternative?*

Rather than relying on your most recent performance, the source of your confidence should be your preparation and skill acquisition. These factors are under your control and are more consistent.

Consider the great confidence a young Navy SEAL takes with him into battle, even if he has no combat experience. The SEAL's confidence is based upon his intense preparation, not upon his prior performance in battle.

We call war "monkey business" because of how easy it is compared to training.

—*Brian "Iron Ed" Hiner, former Navy SEAL and author of* First, Fast, Fearless

---

Have You Ever Seen Jesus?

Chad Bradford was a relief pitcher for the Oakland A's from 2001–2004. Under Rick's tutelage, he became one of the dominant setup relievers in the American League. He did so without a blazing fastball. His fastball was in the mid-80-mph range— very slow for a big leaguer. To be successful, Bradford relied on deception. With his unconventional submarine-style delivery, his knuckles almost scraped the ground as he released the ball toward home plate.

Chad shared with me a funny conversation Rick had with him to move him from doubting to confident.[2]

> In 2001, the *Moneyball* season and my first season with Oakland, Rick made some big changes to my mechanics in spring training that really helped me and gave me a lot of confidence. I had pitched well most of the year, but in August, I had a stretch with a couple bad outings in a row. I was struggling with my confidence. It was my greatest weakness. When things weren't going well, I had zero self-confidence.

All the pitchers that believe they can and all the pitchers that believe they can't are right.

—Rick Peterson, borrowing from the famous quote by Henry Ford

---

> Rick pulled me aside and asked, "What's going on?"
>
> I told Rick, "I don't know. My stuff just isn't there right now. I'm getting hit. I don't know what's going on. I don't feel like I can pitch consistently right now. I don't feel like I can get guys out. I don't know if it's my mechanics."

Rick tells me, "Chad, your mechanics are just fine. You're just doubting yourself."

And I said, "Maybe you're right. Maybe I'm just doubting myself. I had a really good stretch of games for a month and then I just hit a wall."

We started talking about my confidence and Rick asks me, "Why don't you believe you can get this done? Why don't you believe you can go out there and get these hitters out?"

I said, "Well, Rick, I don't know. If I could answer that question, I wouldn't be in this predicament."

Rick thinks for a minute and then asks me, "Are you a Christian?"

Rick knows I am a Christian. He knows what's important to all of his pitchers. I went along with him: "Yes Rick, I am."

"So you're telling me you believe in Jesus Christ?"

"Absolutely, 100 percent."

"Hey, have you ever seen him?"

"No Rick, I've never seen Jesus."

"Have you ever seen yourself pitch well on video?"

"Yes, I have seen myself pitch well."

"Rick starts laughing and says,

How in the world can you believe in Jesus Christ and you've never seen him and you've seen yourself pitch great for months and you don't believe you can get hitters out?

It was so simple. Rick boosted my confidence. It was hard to argue with his logic.

Chad closed his conversation with me by saying,

> I want you to know about the major impact Rick has had on my life. When I first came up to the big leagues in Oakland, Rick improved both my mechanics and my mental approach. He taught me how to be successful in the major leagues. After we both left Oakland for different teams following the 2004 season, I got injured and didn't pitch much in 2005. When I did pitch, I didn't pitch well.
>
> In 2006, when I had the chance to be reunited with Rick and play for the New York Mets, it was a no-brainer. In New York, he got me back on track. I had a great year and we went to the playoffs. Right after that season, I signed a three-year, $10.5 million deal with Baltimore. My family is financially secure because of what Rick did to get me back on track.

> **When you have doubts because of a poor recent performance, refocus on the skills you've acquired during your preparation *and* relive your best past performances.**

In order to relive your best past performances, you need to be able to remember these performances. Shortly after you've finished celebrating a great performance, capture your thoughts and feelings in writing—specifically what you did, the outcome that resulted, and how it made you feel.

If you have videos of your best performances, save them. Create a personal highlight reel of your best moments. Break the poor performance/low confidence cycle by revisiting these resources. It's amazing how powerful and confident you feel after reliving your best performances and the feelings associated with them.

You Don't Have to Feel Great to Perform Great

Hall of Fame starting pitcher Tom Glavine, who has the seventh most wins for a left-hander in baseball history, shared a number of things in our conversation that surprised me. For one, he told me he rarely felt like he had his "A" game (i.e., was in the zone) when he pitched.[3]

Tommy, as his teammates called him, told me he liked to look at his season in five-start segments. This was his way of chunking his season of thirty-five starts down to a more manageable number.

> One time out of those five starts, you're probably going to go out there and everything is going to be great, you're going to feel good, you're going to have your good stuff, have your good location, and that's the game you should go out there and pitch a shutout or something close to it.

> The other four times, something's going to be missing. Whether you don't feel good physically or you don't have your good fastball or you don't have your good command or you don't have your good movement. The chances are something is going to be a little bit off, so you better figure it out.

> If the only time you can win is when you go out there and all the stars are aligned and everything is great, then you're going to struggle because that's just not reality. You're not going to go out there and have everything going exactly the way you want it to go every time you go out there. So you better figure something out on those other nights.

> In 1991, my career took off. That was my first 20-win season and my first Cy Young Award. The biggest difference that year was I learned to how to win games when I didn't have

my "A" stuff (best pitches working for me). I learned how to win that B+ game or that C+ game (where I was pitching less than my best). That really made all the difference in not only that season, but in the seasons going forward because now I have confidence I can go out there and win when I'm not at my best.

It's hard to believe, but a Hall of Famer indicated he was "in the zone" only one out of every five starts over the course of his career. If Glavine was in the zone only 20 percent of the time, then how realistic is it that we will find ourselves in the zone more often?

The reality is we don't always bring our best to work each day. The multitude of reasons may include lack of sleep, family issues, health issues, excessive workload, conflict with colleagues, lack of confidence, or apathy toward certain aspects of our work. Yet, despite these challenges, we're still expected to perform with excellence.

So now that I know I'm out of the zone much more often than I'm in the zone, how can I learn to perform well and win, even when I don't feel my best and am not bringing my "A" game?

Glavine again offers us insight. "If I went out there on a given night and I didn't have my good fastball, then what? I felt like I had other pitches or movement I could rely on. I knew I had put in the work in the bullpen and gotten to the point where I could make the adjustments."

In other words, Glavine wasn't one dimensional. His preparation helped him develop an arsenal of pitches he could throw with precision. When one of his pitches wasn't working, he adjusted. In addition, when his physical talent was not at its peak, Glavine used his mind to outsmart hitters.

> ### You don't have to feel great to perform great.

Travel in Time

When we are in the midst of a pressure situation, we can feel trapped with no way to escape. However, changing the context of a situation often changes how we perceive the situation and its meaning. One way to change context, and the options you can identify, is to look at a situation from a different point in time.

Z Travels to Field 2[4]

Left-handed starting pitcher Barry Zito was selected by the Oakland A's with the ninth pick in the first round of the 1999 draft. Zito signed for a $1.59 million bonus and began his professional career in the minor leagues with the Visalia Oaks, Oakland's class A team. He was promoted to the Oakland AA team and then finished the season with just one start with the AAA team.

In the spring of 2000, Zito was not expected to make the major league team. As is the case with most young pitchers, even high draft choices, Zito was expected to continue getting valuable experience in AAA before being ready to pitch in the big leagues.

Zito's invite to spring training in 2000 was an opportunity for him to get a taste of major league play in a low-pressure environment. Despite thriving in spring training and exceeding the A's expectations of him, Zito started the regular season as planned with the AAA team.

On July 22, 2000, Zito, nicknamed "Z" by his teammates, was called up to Oakland and made his big league debut against the Anaheim Angels. He pitched well through the first four innings, giving up just one run. When he went out to the mound to start the 5th inning, he knew he was eligible for his first major league win if he could finish the inning with Oakland keeping the lead. That seemed like an easy task, considering his team had staked him to a 7–1 lead.

But the more you think about the outcome, the easier it is to get distracted from the process—hitting the glove—that it takes to get to that outcome. That's what happened to Z. He started the 5th inning by walking Adam Kennedy, giving up a single to Darin Erstad, and walking Benji Gil. The bases were loaded with nobody out. The Angels' best three hitters—Mo Vaughn, Tim Salmon, and Garrett Anderson—were next. Suddenly, Z's first win was in doubt. A's pitching coach Rick Peterson jogged to the mound.

Rick said to Z, "Do you remember what I told you on Field 2 in spring training earlier this year?" At the Oakland spring training complex, there are multiple fields that are numbered.

Z responded, "Yeah, on Field 2 when I was nervous, you told me to just relax and act like I was surfing a wave out there. Nice and easy."

Rick knew Z had grown up in southern California, that he enjoyed surfing, and that it relaxed him.

Rick's advice to relax by traveling to another place and time had worked for Z on Field 2 in spring training. Would it help him relax in his major league debut and get out of the jam?

Z did relax and he also drew on the confidence he gained by pitching well on Field 2 months earlier in spring training. Then he proceeded to strike out Mo Vaughn, Tim Salmon, and Garrett Anderson to end the inning and the Angels' threat. Zito earned the win in his major league debut.

Mo Goes Back in Time[5]

Mariano Rivera, nicknamed Mo, is the best closer in the history of baseball. Mo's initial role with the New York Yankees was as a *setup man*. A setup man is a relief pitcher often responsible for pitching the game's 7th and 8th innings. The role of the setup man is to preserve a lead for his team before the ball is handed over to the closer, typically in the 9th inning. The role of the closer is to preserve the lead in the 9th inning when the pressure is greatest. The closer is typically the best relief pitcher on the team. More than any other role, it requires nerves of steel.

In 1996, Mo proved to be such a good pitcher for the Yankees as a setup man that the team decided to let its closer, John Wetteland, sign with the Texas Rangers as a free agent during the off season. At the start of the 1997 season, Hall of Fame manager Joe Torre inserted Mo into the high-pressure closer's role.

In his autobiography, *The Closer*, Mo says, "I minimize the difference in the roles publicly, insisting I feel no added pressure, but the truth is I *do* feel pressure. I want to prove the Yankees did the right thing. I want to show everybody I can do it. I want not only to be as good as John Wetteland. I want to be better than him."

The '97 season did not start well. Mo blew three of his first six save opportunities. Through the first nine innings of the season, he gave up fourteen hits and four runs. He performed much worse as a closer than he did as a setup man.

Two things helped Mo turn his performance around. First, Mel Stottlemyre and Joe Torre, the pitching coach and manager of the Yankees respectively, spoke with Mo. "Mo, you know what you need to do? You need to be Mariano Rivera. That's all. Nothing more, nothing less. It looks to us like you're trying to be perfect. You're our closer. You're our guy, and we want you to be our guy, and that is not going to change," Torre told him. Mo felt an immediate sense of relief. "As I walked out of his office, I felt about 10,000 tons lighter."

The second thing that helped turn Mo's performance around was a reframe that relieved the pressure he felt as a closer. He pretended he was again pitching in the 7th or 8th inning where he felt so comfortable rather than pitching the pressure-packed 9th inning. "I've had a great deal of success since the end of 1995 in getting big league hitters out. It doesn't matter what inning it is. So why change anything? Why focus differently? That's what I need to keep in mind."

Mo changed the context, picturing himself at a different place in time, albeit only one or two innings earlier. The payoff from the reframe and the meeting with Torre and Stottlemyre was immediate. Mo proceeded to run off 12 straight saves.

Mo served as the Yankees closer for 17 seasons, ending his career in 2013. He is a 13-time All-Star, 5-time World Series champion, and Major League Baseball's career leader in saves (652) and games finished (952). Mo is widely regarded as the most dominant relief pitcher in major league history.

> Leave the present pressure situation and picture yourself performing in a time and place where you had great success.

Two Lists to Move from Weakness and Uncertainty to Strength[6]

When we're under pressure, often we focus on our doubts and fail to recognize our strengths. In some cases, our doubts arise from a perceived weakness. In other cases, we have doubts because of the uncertainty of the situation. In either case, we can regain our confidence by shifting our focus back on our strengths and the actions we will take.

During one of my conversations with sports psychologist Dr. Julie Bell (a.k.a. Dr. J), I shared that my son Cole was about a month away from hockey tryouts. Cole's Caveman was in full gear. He felt fear, worry, and doubt for a variety of reasons, including but not limited to the fact that he didn't know the coach. In addition, his speed and agility were not as good as some of the other players.

Dr. J recommended Cole pull out a sheet of paper and make two lists. On one side of the paper, Cole was to list all of his strengths. Here is the list Cole made:

- Strong shot
- Quick, accurate passes to get the puck out of the zone
- Smart decision-making, when to take chances and when to play it safe
- Give great effort
- Coachable
- In great shape
- Good teammate
- Physical strength
- Use my body to shield the puck from attackers

On the other side of the paper, Cole was to list the top three or four things that were causing him to be anxious. But he wasn't to stop there. For each of the three or four things causing him to be anxious, he was to write down the actions he could take to address his anxiety. Here is the second list Cole made:

- I don't know the coach and he doesn't know me.
  - Listen to the coach and do what he says.
  - Give good effort from start to finish.
  - Give coach a fist bump and thank him at the end of practice.
- My feet need to be quicker.
  - Practice using the speed ladder.

- Practice my stride and foot quickness using the slide board.
- Shuttle run, sprints, forward, back, and side to side.
- Jump rope.
- My puck handling isn't as good as I want it to be.
  - Practice each day in the basement for 20 minutes or more. Practice the same moves coach has taught us in practice.
- As I'm traveling to the rink, I get nervous.
  - Pray.
  - Take deep breaths.
  - Visualize specific things I want to do in the defensive, neutral, and offensive zones of the ice.
  - Laugh by watching the Will Ferrell "We gotta keep our composure!" video (*https://www.youtube.com/watch?v= oydv8lFPeIY*).

By identifying and then taking specific actions to address specific concerns, Cole was able to tame his Caveman and move from feeling anxious to feeling confident he was doing what was under his control.

List the strengths you bring to the situation; reduce the pressure by listing your fears, worries, and doubts and the specific actions you will take to address them.

Highlights

- Basing your confidence on your most recent performance is dangerous. Your performance will fluctuate. You will have good days and bad days. You need a more consistent source of confidence, one that is under your control. Base your confidence on your preparation, not on your performance.

- Too many of us assume we have to feel great to perform great. The reality is we will only feel "in the zone" a small percentage of the time. Think of Tommy: You don't have to feel great to perform great.

- When we are in the midst of a pressure situation, we can feel trapped with no way to escape. However, we can relieve the pressure by taking ourselves to another place and time. Think of Z going back to Field 2 in spring training during his major league debut. Think of Mo going to the relaxed 7th inning instead of the 9th-inning pressure cooker.

- We often doubt ourselves because we focus on our weaknesses or concerns and fail to recognize our strengths. Think of Dr. J's two lists—one to capture relevant strengths and the other to identify the actions you'll take to address your doubts.

Try This

- Identify a pressure situation where you have doubts you will come through at crunch time. Try one or more of the following to boost your confidence:

  - Remember you don't need to feel great to perform great.

  - Recall your hours of preparation. If it helps, total up the number of hours you've prepared for this situation.

  - Travel to a time and place in the past when you performed very well and picture yourself there in the present.

  - Make two lists: one list of your strengths that will help you perform well in this situation, and another list with the actions you will take to overcome your fear, worry, and doubt.

7

Reframing from Failure to a Learning Moment™1

Baseball teaches us how to deal with failure. We learn at a very young age that failure is the norm in baseball and, precisely because we have failed, we hold in high regard those who fail less often—those who hit safely in one out of three chances and become star players.

—*FAY VINCENT, former Commissioner of Baseball*

Using New Language to Kick-Start the Reframing of a Tribe's Thinking[2]

I met Garry Ridge, President and CEO of the WD-40 Company, about ten years ago after he spoke at The Ken Blanchard Companies' client conference. During that conference, Garry shared the concept this chapter was named after—learning moments. Since that time, I've had the good fortune to speak with Garry on a few occasions. Most recently, Garry shared with me how he improves his own performance as well as the performance of the larger WD-40 Company "tribe" by reframing.

It started when I looked at WD-40 in the late 1990s. We were seeking to grow from $90 million to $400 million in revenue. I thought about what could keep us from hitting our growth targets. From my perspective, it boiled down to one thing—fear.

Fear is the most paralyzing emotion you can have. We needed to transition our culture from fear to freedom. In our case, we needed to eliminate the fear of sharing knowledge, especially about our failures.

At the time, the currency of WD-40 was knowledge. The more knowledge someone had, the more power they had. I realized people were keeping this knowledge hidden in silos and not sharing it because they were afraid. The prevailing thought was, "The more I know, the safer I am. If I keep this as my currency of power, I'll be safer than anybody else." I knew if we were going to quadruple in size, we had to get that knowledge out and into the organization.

One of the ways we began shifting people's thinking, and then our culture, was through the use of new language.

Different words enable people to think differently.

We choose to use certain words with great intention.

For example, in many organizations, people use the word "team." The problem with teams is they are temporary. Teams may win games or championships, but they don't typically stay together for a long time.

I'm a native Aussie and I have great respect and admiration for our indigenous tribes. The reasons are many. In contrast to a team, a tribe is enduring. A tribe also creates a stronger feeling of belonging, which is a basic human motivator. In addition, the biggest responsibility of a tribal leader is to share his knowledge with the rest of the tribe—where to find food, how to stay safe, essentially how to survive. Tribal leaders are revered and recognized as powerful because of the knowledge they share with the rest of the tribe. When our employees began to think of sharing knowledge and learning as tribe leaders and members do, this new language and way of thinking helped us remove the fear of sharing knowledge.

We also needed to take the fear out of mistakes. Most people look at mistakes as career-damaging events rather than opportunities to learn. Therefore, they cover up mistakes in the hope no one finds out. What I needed to do was to help people realize mistakes were inevitable but not necessarily fatal. To do that, I had to redefine the concept of *mistakes*.

When things go wrong, we don't call them *mistakes*.

We call them *learning moments*. A learning moment is the positive or negative outcome of any situation, openly shared for the benefit of all.

In addition to the shift in language, we needed to teach people not to be afraid to fail. Our leaders had to earn our tribe members' trust by showing neither I nor any of our tribal leaders would take adverse action if someone tried something new and didn't succeed. These days, we look at missteps as learning opportunities. We applaud the chance to learn and grow and incorporate new knowledge into their work.

One example of a learning moment is our experience launching a new line of specialty maintenance products designed exclusively for industrial users. We wanted to extend our brand without hurting our core WD-40 brand. We had research pointing to the need for a unique brand. So we created a new brand called BLUE WORKS. Each product in the BLUE WORKS brand came with a "BLUE WORKS" logo; the WD-40 shield you see on all consumer products was not included. The bottom of the can contained a small WD-40 company logo to show BLUE WORKS came from the same trusted source as the WD-40 shield.

The BLUE WORKS brand did not come close to meeting our expectations. We underestimated the power of the shield. That was a learning moment that cost us a lot of money, but there were no dead bodies on the road. As a result of our learning, we switched from BLUE WORKS to WD-40 Specialist and included the powerful WD-40 shield. With the switch in brands, sales jumped from $2 million to $20 million, with long-term opportunity estimated at $125 million.

Learning moments can be things you learn from positive outcomes and, just as importantly, things you learn from negative outcomes. They each have value, but learning moments from negative outcomes usually aren't really comfortable to share. We started socializing the idea of learning moments. We set up a monthly recognition program for tribe members to share their learning moments. The grand prize at the end of the year was a trip around the world to share the learning moments with tribe members in other offices. In the first month, we only had a few entries. We made heroes of them, cheering them on. We got more entries each passing month. We were talking about learning moments regularly. It is now embedded as part of what we do.

It's hard to argue with the results of these and other similar culture- and performance-enhancing reframes. Under Garry's leadership, WD-40 Company's revenues have more than tripled, from $100 million to $380 million. And the WD-40 tribe of 430 people worldwide accomplished this feat while making it a great place to work.

Every two years, tribe members complete a survey that ranks their degree of engagement—how delighted they are with the WD-40 Company work environment, with their leaders, and with their peers. In 2016, WD-40 Company had an overall engagement score of 92.8 percent. An incredible 98.4 percent of tribe members indicated they love to tell people they work for WD-40 and an astonishing 99.1 percent of tribe members said their opinions and values are a good fit with the WD-40 Company culture.

There's a famous story told about Tom Watson, the founder of IBM. One of his subordinates had made a horrendous mistake that had cost the company ten million dollars. He was called into Watson's office and said, "I suppose you want my resignation." Watson looked at him and said, "Are you kidding? We just spent ten million dollars educating you."

There's a valuable lesson in everything that happens. The best leaders are the ones who learn the lesson and put the most empowering frame on outside events.[3]

—*Tony Robbins*

Does Feedback Make You Bitter or Better? [4, 5, 6]

More than most endeavors in life, baseball is riddled with failure. Hitters are considered great if they get a hit just three times out of ten. The baseball box score serves as a daily performance report, highlighting the successes and failures of every player. In the case of major leaguers, their failures are on display publicly to fans in the thousands and sometimes millions.

While all baseball players know no one succeeds all of the time, the best players have figured out how to respond to the inevitable failures in a way that makes them better.

Tom Glavine pitched 16 seasons with the Atlanta Braves, winning a total of 244 games, including 5 seasons of 20 wins or more (the gold standard for a starting pitcher) and 2 seasons in which he won the Cy Young Award as the best pitcher in the National League. At the rate he was winning, Glavine looked like a sure thing to surpass 300 wins and earn his place in the baseball Hall of Fame.

At the end of the 2002 season, Glavine's contract with Atlanta was up. Glavine surprised many in baseball by leaving the only professional team he'd ever played for and signing with the New York Mets. He signed a three-year contract for $35 million, with an option for a fourth year that could make the deal worth $42.5 million.

It would be an understatement to say expectations in New York were high. These expectations came from many sources—the team, the New York fans and media, and Glavine himself.

Baseball analysts projected Glavine would reach the magic 300 win total as a Met sometime during the 2006 season and lift the Mets to glory in the process. Then, a not-so-funny thing happened on Glavine's road to the Hall of Fame. He struggled.

In 2003, Glavine finished the season with 9 wins and 14 losses. This was the first time since his rookie season he hadn't won at least 10 games. *Had he lost his skills?* No. *Was he buckling under the pressure of playing in New York?* No. The game had changed.

Major League Baseball introduced the QuesTec Umpire Information System. QuesTec is a pitch-tracking technology used to evaluate the performance of home plate umpires. It keeps track of how many correct and incorrect ball and strike calls an umpire has during a game.

While he was in Atlanta, Glavine had thrived for years with one approach—pitch to the outside part of the plate, preferably off the plate, to get hitters to chase pitches outside the strike zone. Because of the success and reputation he'd earned in Atlanta, umpires often called pitches that were just off the outside edge of home plate a strike for Glavine. Now that the umpires were being evaluated more objectively, they stopped giving Glavine that strike and started calling a pitch in the same location a ball.

This meant Glavine's game plan to get hitters to chase his pitch off the plate no longer worked.

As Glavine put the tough 2003 season behind him and prepared for a turnaround season in 2004, Rick made a huge decision to leave the Oakland A's. Despite the great success of the A's pitching staff and the team, Rick wanted to move back to the East Coast so he could be a bigger part of his sons' lives. The New York Mets hired Rick as their new pitching coach.

Glavine started the 2004 season like the pitcher he was during his years in Atlanta. He was superb. He made his ninth All-Star team that July. Unfortunately, disaster struck Glavine—literally—in early August. He was involved in a crash while riding in the back of a cab on the way to Shea Stadium. He tried to return to pitching too soon after the injury and pitched poorly. More than ever, Glavine's career-long quest for 300 career wins now looked like it was in jeopardy.

The 2005 season began the same way 2004 finished, with Glavine struggling mightily. To add to the pressure, the New York media called the free agent signing of Glavine a big mistake. One radio talk show host wondered if the driver who had hit Glavine's cab the year before could be found to hit him again.[7]

On a June road trip to the West Coast, Glavine's pitching hit rock bottom. He faced the Seattle Mariners and gave up six runs in less than three innings. For the season, Glavine had just four wins against seven losses and had given up a dismal average of more than five earned runs per game.

It was eating Glavine alive to pitch so poorly. He wasn't the only one. Rick agonized as well. Rick had so much respect for Glavine as both a pitcher and a person.

Glavine was used to no longer getting the pitch off the outside corner of the plate called a strike because of the QuesTec Umpire Information System. The problem was he hadn't figured out how to adjust.

On the long plane ride home from Seattle, Rick decided it was the right time to challenge Glavine to change. He was not going to ask Glavine to make a small change. He was about to ask him to blow up the way he had pitched for 18 years and try something he had never done as a pro. Not an easy conversation.

Rick knew the recipient of feedback and change often feels threatened. He knew he needed to reframe the conversation as an opportunity for Glavine to get back on track in his quest for 300 wins.

Rick got up out of his seat near the front of the plane, ordered a couple beers from the flight attendant, and walked to the back of the plane where Glavine was sitting. He slid into the empty seat next to Glavine and cracked open the beers. Knowing Glavine was an avid golfer, Rick decided to use a golf analogy. He asked, "Tommy, how many clubs are you allowed to have in your golf bag?"

Understandably so, Glavine wasn't in a great mood, but he respected Rick enough to play along. "Fourteen," Glavine answered.

Rick responded, "Right, and right now you're only using two of the clubs in your bag—fastball outside and change up outside. Every team in the league has the same scouting report on you: lay off the pitch off the outside edge of the plate; wait for you to pitch over the plate, and then take the ball to the opposite field or up the middle. They're sitting on your pitches. You were successful in the past by keeping guys off balance. No one is off balance right now."

Glavine could be bitter about what he was hearing or he could learn from it. He couldn't argue with what Rick was saying, but he wasn't sure what to do about it to get better.

Rick shared his idea: "You've got to start using the other clubs in your bag. You have to start pitching inside!"

Glavine looked at Rick in disbelief. "Pitch inside? Me?" For a non-power pitcher like Glavine, pitching inside was risky. If a hitter is ready for an inside pitch, he's likely to crush it for a home run.

The two men talked further about when to pitch inside and with what pitches, and when to go back to the outside of the plate. At the end of the conversation, Glavine thought, "I can't pitch any worse. Why not try it?"

The new Glavine pitched in Yankee Stadium a few nights later. He pitched both inside and outside. Yankees manager Joe Torre remembered, "He was a different guy completely. I was tempted to check his uniform number to make sure it was Tom."[8] Glavine won the game, pitching as well as he had all season.

After the game, Glavine said, "They knew I was willing to come inside, but they didn't know when I was going to come inside. It was like the old days; I had them chasing again."

Glavine's turnaround was extraordinary. Following his conversation on the plane with Rick, Glavine gave up an average of half as many earned runs per game for the remainder of the season. From 2005–2007, Glavine won 41 games, winning his 300th game on August 5, 2007. On July 27, 2014, Glavine was inducted into the National Baseball Hall of Fame. During his induction speech, Glavine recognized Rick for the help he provided.[9]

Rick Peterson, later in my career with the Mets, you helped me to reinvent myself and make the changes I needed to make for the latter part of my career. Trust me, when you're doing something for 16 or 17 years, it's not an easy thing to change. But you talked me into it, you convinced me of it, and you gave me confidence to do it. Rick Peterson, thanks so much for your help.

Like all of us, Glavine encountered adversity. He received feedback that his performance wasn't up to his own standards or the standards of others. Like us, he had to ask himself: *Am I going to be bitter about the feedback I'm receiving or am I going to learn from it and act on it to get better? What opportunity might I miss if I choose to disregard this feedback?*

Feedback is the Breakfast of Champions.
                                        —*Dr. Ken Blanchard, leadership guru*

Fixed Mindset or Growth Mindset?

One of the most influential books I read during my research for this book is Carol Dweck's *Mindset: The New Psychology of Success*. I highly encourage you to read it as just sharing its big idea within this section will not do it justice. Dweck's research teaches us that the view you adopt of yourself—your mindset—profoundly affects the way you lead your life and the success you will or will not achieve.

Your mindset is the view you have of your qualities and characteristics, where they come from and whether they can change.

Dweck juxtaposes two different mindsets at opposite ends of the spectrum—the fixed mindset and the growth mindset.

A *fixed mindset* comes from the belief that your qualities are carved in stone. Who you are is who you are. Characteristics such as intelligence, creativity, and athletic ability are fixed traits rather than something that can be developed.[10]

The fixed mindset leads to a desire to prove yourself over and over. Your self-worth is tightly linked with your performance. Challenges are seen as threats, something to be avoided. Criticism is seen as an attack on your character, also to be avoided.

In contrast, a *growth mindset* comes from the belief that your qualities are things you can cultivate through effort. While people differ greatly in temperament, aptitude, talents, and interests, everyone can change and grow through application and experience. In other words, people with a growth mindset see themselves as a work in progress.

Having a growth mindset encourages learning and effort. It leads you to embrace challenges because you don't see them as threats but as opportunities to learn. If you truly believe you can improve at something, you will be much more driven to learn and practice. An objective critique of your performance is seen as valuable feedback and openly embraced. The hallmark of the growth mindset is the passion for sticking with it, *especially* when things are *not* going well.

Your mindset has a critical effect on how you view pressure situations. As you've likely surmised by now, people with a fixed mindset put a lot of pressure on themselves. They avoid performing under pressure or give up easily when they face the inevitable adversity or setbacks. In contrast, people with a growth mindset embrace pressure situations, recognize they won't be perfect, and continue to learn and improve.

While Dweck writes about these two mindsets as an either-or for simplicity sake, it's possible to have a fixed mindset in one area of your life and a growth mindset in another area. For example, I have a fixed mindset when it comes to my ability to dance. I see myself as having little to no ability and almost no chance of improving. I avoid dancing like the plague. In contrast, I have a growth mindset when it comes to my ability to golf. I realize I am a work in progress and am excited to continue practicing and improving.

Whatever mindset you have in a given area of your life will guide you and your success in that area. Based on my current fixed mindset around dancing, you won't see me on *Dancing with the Stars* or even a local dance floor anytime soon. In contrast, you will see me regularly practicing my golf game, aspiring to one day compete for a club championship.

The best part about what Dweck shares about mindsets? If you have a fixed mindset, it isn't fixed. Anyone, including you, can learn to develop a growth mindset!

> When things don't go your way, ask yourself this:
>
> *What can I learn from this to decrease the likelihood it will happen again?*

What's Your Explanatory Style?

I was speaking with a friend and colleague, Lisa Zigarmi, and sharing some of what I've learned about reframing pressure. I knew Lisa would not only be interested in what I was sharing, but she would be able to advance my thinking. She received her master's degree in Applied Positive Psychology, studying under the famous Martin (Marty) Seligman at University of Pennsylvania. Lisa shared with me Seligman's concept of *learned optimism*.

Seligman came to the concept of learned optimism by initially studying learned helplessness. He ran experiments that subjected participants to recurring undesirable outcomes. As expected, some participants blamed themselves and gave up. What interested Seligman most, however, were the other participants who resisted becoming pessimistic and helpless. Why didn't these participants blame themselves or give up? The answer was optimism.

Seligman's follow-up experiments shifted from helplessness to teaching people how to become optimists. This teaching requires people to challenge their negative self-talk and think about their reactions to adversity in a new way. That sounds an awful lot like reframing under pressure.

The big difference between pessimists and optimists is in their *explanatory style* of adverse situations. Their explanatory style differs in three key areas—permanence, pervasiveness, and personalization—the Three P's for short.[11]

Permanence Optimists believe bad events to be more temporary than permanent and bounce back quickly from failure. ("This is just one performance; I'll have plenty of other opportunities to display my skills.") In contrast, pessimists point to permanent causes for bad events and may take longer to recover. ("I'll never be able to do this; I don't know why I even try.")

To show that optimists have the best of both worlds, optimists also believe good things happen for reasons that are permanent. ("My skills are excellent; I can't wait to do this again.") To show that pessimists have the worst of both worlds, they believe good things happen for reasons that are temporary. ("I got lucky.")

Pervasiveness Optimists compartmentalize helplessness. ("I didn't get the outcome I wanted at this, but I will when I try something else.") Pessimists assume failure in one area of life means failure in life as a whole. ("I can't do anything right.") Optimists also allow good events to brighten every area of their lives rather than just the particular area in which the event occurred. ("Life is good; I'm on a roll.")

Personalization   Optimists blame bad events on causes outside of themselves. ("I didn't get the outcome I wanted this time because I was unlucky.") Pessimists blame themselves for events that occur. ("I am a failure.")

Please note Rick and I are big believers in taking personal responsibility for the factors under your control. We don't recommend shifting blame to others when bad events occur. Personalization simply highlights that pessimists tend to blame themselves for everything, even those factors well outside their control. This is very detrimental to performance.

Based on the Three P's, good events provide optimists with a huge boost in confidence and bad events don't diminish the optimist's confidence. In contrast, good events do not provide pessimists with a boost in confidence, but bad events damage the pessimist's confidence. It's the worst of both worlds for a pessimist and the best of both worlds for an optimist.

The following story shares how one leader was able to apply the skill of reframing via learned optimism to move from threat to opportunity.

From Nightmare to Success

Susan Torroella is a dynamic and successful leader. She has a track record of awards, including but not limited to receiving Fortune Small Business's Boss of the Year, being an Ernst & Young Entrepreneur of the Year finalist, and being one of PharmaVoice's 100 Most Inspiring Leaders in Life Sciences.

As you might expect from a leader of this caliber, Susan knows pressure. She was the CEO of Columbia MedCom Group from 2001 to 2009. She recently spoke with executive leadership coach, Lelia O'Connor, about pressures she's faced. In Susan's own words, she thrives on pressures such as deadlines and speaking in front of large groups of people. She calls these "mini pressures." She also tells the story of the single greatest pressure she's ever faced—having her company go under.

> I had bought out the prior owners of the company. I wanted to provide jobs for people and create an amazing culture. The company was my legacy. For years, we were enormously successful and winning awards like *Baltimore* magazine's Best Places to Work. In 2008, the economy contracted, negatively impacting our business and many others. Even though we weren't connected to Lehman Brothers in any way, when they went under, it set off a chain reaction. Investors everywhere were concerned. Some panicked.

> Our investor called the note on our loan, telling us we needed to close the company and give all our assets to them as partial payment. It was two weeks before Christmas when I got the letter forcing my company into foreclosure. It was a nightmare. I had invested everything into this company—my money, my time, and my heart. It was my dream. Now it was crushed.

> As I look back, in the months leading up to the end, there were parts I definitely didn't handle well. The nightmare was so enormous to me that I couldn't sleep. I'm talking all night long for multiple days in a row. As a result, I couldn't think straight. To add fuel to the fire, I wasn't eating and was losing a lot of weight.

> There were a number of things that helped me turn the corner and move from threat to opportunity. I had a great support system. My mother gave me perspective, telling me

over and over, "Everything will be okay." She helped me see that, as awful as I was feeling, my children weren't going to go hungry and we weren't going to be homeless.

I also found relief and optimism after reading through a profile in *Fast Company* of a highly successful leader. In the profile, the leader mentioned very matter-of-factly, "My business went under and now I'm doing this." It made me realize that, in our society, we don't talk about failure. But all of these really successful people have failed many times and then went on to do great things. I realized this was temporary and I could do the same. I've reinvented myself in another career (note: Susan is currently serving as executive vice president at Wellness Corporate Solutions). I've adopted the mantra that...

A setback just sets up your next comeback.

The leader profile in *Fast Company* also helped me to stop taking the loss so personally. I am not a failure. I did not bring on the financial crisis that caused our lender to call our note and force us to close our business. This business endeavor simply didn't survive for a variety of reasons, many of which were out of my control.

Another thing I learned to do was not to let the business going under affect how I performed in other areas of my life, like parenting. In fact, we used the business going under as a learning moment to teach our kids lessons on perspective and how to manage finances.

Once I got past the initial shock that I couldn't stop the foreclosure and everyone was going to lose their jobs, I redefined what success looked like in this situation. For us, success was servicing our clients in the best way possible, right until the very last minute. Success was also going through mock interviews and helping every employee get a job.

As I think back on that situation that was the toughest pressure I have faced in my life, I realize anything I'm facing in the present seems miniscule in comparison. I have lots of confidence because, if I got through that, and I did, I can get through anything.

The optimist's outlook on undesirable events:

What happened was an unlucky situation [not personal], and really just a setback [not permanent] for this one, of many, goals [not pervasive].[12]
—*Martin Seligman, educator and author of* Learned Optimism

Highlights

- To eliminate the fear of failure and sharing knowledge about failures, choose new words. Different words can help people to think differently and then act differently. Like Garry Ridge and WD-40, reframe from failure to learning moment.

- There is a valuable lesson in everything that happens. Those who rebound fastest from adversity are the ones who learn the lesson and make the necessary adjustment to their thoughts and actions.

- Baseball players get feedback daily about their successes and their inevitable failures. The box score is a daily performance report. Fans boo or applaud. Coaches limit or increase playing time. Just like these players, you have a choice about what to do with feedback—get bitter or get better.

- Adopt a growth mindset. Recognize you are a work in progress. Embrace pressure situations, recognizing you won't be perfect, and continually seek to learn and improve.

- Like Susan Torroella, respond to undesirable outcomes with learned optimism. Reframe your view of these undesirable outcomes as temporary, limited to a given situation, and not a reflection of your value as a person (i.e., not permanent, not pervasive, not personal).

Try This

- Reflect on how you typically respond to undesirable outcomes. Consider whether this response is hurting or helping future performance.

- Ask yourself:

  - *What am I learning from these situations? How can I change my mindset now?*

  - *How does this inform how I'll prepare for similar situations in the future? How will I seize an opportunity from a disaster?*

  - *Does my new game plan give me confidence that I will perform better at my next opportunity?*

8

Reframing from Prepared to Overprepared

Talent does not equal performance. Preparation equals performance.

—*RICK PETERSON (with an Assist from Michael Jordan)*

During the proposal phase of this book, I spoke with Neal Maillet, our executive editor at Berrett-Koehler. Neal asked me to share with him the number one reframe I've learned that helps me perform better under pressure. My answer was easy. Move from what I used to consider good preparation to preparing like an elite performer under pressure.

Neal challenged me and asked me to think twice about whether we should include a chapter on preparation. He said everyone already knows they have to prepare. He's correct *and* I pushed hard to have it included because of what I've learned during my research and application. Namely, that many don't know the difference between preparing to perform for low to moderate pressure and preparing for intense pressure.

In fact, there is a different type of preparation that's needed to more consistently come through at crunch time. Run-of-the-mill preparation under the crucible of pressure is not enough. When it comes to performing under pressure, if you're not overprepared, then you're actually underprepared. The best performers at crunch time engage in *tougher than you'll ever need* preparation.

You may be thinking, *In Chapter 3, you coached me to Try Easy. Now it sounds like you're coaching me to try harder. Which is it?* It's actually both, so it's important to clarify the timing of when you should be trying harder versus trying easier. During the preparation phase, it's important to reach the level where you can perform without thinking, reaching unconscious competence. This typically involves trying harder. Then, once your big moment arrives—the presentation, the final exam, the musical, the big game—it's time to trust your preparation and try easier. Prepare harder, perform easier.

Based on my lengthy track record of strong performance as a student, an athlete, and a businessman, I thought I knew what good preparation looked like. I was wrong. The reality was that my version of good preparation worked well under conditions of low to moderate pressure. However, I did not know what is needed to consistently perform with excellence under the highest-pressure situations. As a result, at various points throughout my life, I've not performed my best when it mattered most.

Now I have a much firmer grasp on the different level of preparation that separates the best under normal conditions from the best under intense pressure. When I compare how I typically prepared to how the best pressure performers prepare, I realized we weren't even in the same ballpark.

Rick is known for many things throughout the major leagues, and at the top of that list is his intense level of preparation. It's one of the reasons Billy Beane hired him. It's why Hall of Famers Tom Glavine and Pedro Martinez and countless others trusted him. One of Rick's favorite mantras is, "Talent doesn't equal performance. Preparation equals performance!" So who taught Rick this invaluable lesson?

A Lesson from Michael Jordan

It just so happens that when Rick was the codirector of the Chicago White Sox sports psychology program, his path crossed with the most famous athlete on the planet. In 1994, Michael Jordan decided to take a sojourn from professional basketball and try his hand at baseball. Rick delivered sports psychology sessions to Michael and other White Sox prospects in the Florida Instructional League. Even though Rick led the session, he recognized the opportunity to learn from Michael.

Rick recalls one of his memorable conversations with Michael. "I asked Michael, 'Was there ever a moment when you realized you were MJ?' By MJ, I meant the type of performer so great he would be known throughout the world by just his initials. As a young coach, I was motivated to find out what made Michael Jordan transform into MJ. Michael said the turning point was after his sophomore year at the University of North Carolina."

In 1982–83, Michael's freshman year at North Carolina, he hit the game-winning jump shot in the NCAA Championship game. In his sophomore season, North Carolina was knocked out of the NCAA tournament's East Regional Final by Georgia. Untapped potential, unfulfilled expectations.

Rick continued sharing his conversation with MJ: "Michael told me the legendary Coach Dean Smith sat him down after his sophomore season and showed him video clips from a number of different practice sessions and games. Coach Smith asked Michael whether specific clips were from his freshman year or from his sophomore year. Coach Smith asked Michael what his takeaway was from seeing the video clips.

"Michael told Coach Smith, 'Freshman year, I prepared great and played great. Sophomore year, I only prepared good and only played good. At that point, I realized *preparation equals performance*. My level of preparation will be the difference in whether I unleash my full potential or not.'"

Rick's lesson from speaking with MJ? "At that moment, I realized my responsibility as a pitching coach was to make sure my staff was fully prepared to unleash their full potential."

Rick's greatest quality, for me, was his preparation. He was a step ahead of other people in his preparation. He spent countless hours watching video, breaking hitters down, and formulating game plans and ways to go about pitching to guys. When we would sit down for a meeting to go over hitters and scouting reports, it was always much easier to trust those conversations with Rick because you knew he had done his homework.[1]

—*Tom Glavine, Hall of Fame pitcher*

> My level of preparation will be the difference in whether or not I unleash my full potential.

It's about the Mental Boost

There are no doubts about the physical, task-related benefits of high-frequency, high-quality repetitions. However, when it comes to this form of overpreparation, most people underestimate the mental benefits.

Overpreparation enables you to quiet your Caveman. It gives you confidence that you can handle anything. When you're confident, you can relax. When you relax, your brain turns on the good internal pharmacy and releases performance-enhancing chemicals.

These performance enhancers increase the probability you'll per-form at the same level as your capabilities under calm conditions.

Boot Barn CEO Jim Conroy describes this mental edge as follows:

> I give a million presentations and speeches. I'm now at the point where I wear a remote microphone, I don't carry any notes, and I casually walk around while I'm presenting. My colleagues say, 'You make it look so easy. How do you present so naturally?' I don't do it naturally. I prepare like crazy. The reason I prepare is a bit of a twist. It's not about memorizing my lines. It's about relaxing. If I'm relaxed, I can present well, but I'm only relaxed if I'm overprepared. I go through the extra preparation so I feel confident enough when I'm up there that I can relax, think clearly, and engage with the audience. The preparation is what I need to put myself in the right state of mind.[2]

Yes, We Are Going to Do It Again...and Again...

In April of 2014, I decided to move my research from the cold of Chicago to the warmth of Sarasota, Florida. Sarasota is the spring training home of the Baltimore Orioles, Rick's current team. The trip would give me a chance to see Rick in action and observe the preseason preparation of those competing for a spot on the team. As we planned what we wanted to accomplish during my trip, Rick told me he would set up a conversation for me with one of his for-mer pupils, Wilson Alvarez.

Wilson, nicknamed Willie by his teammates, grew up as a star pitcher in Venezuela. As an amateur, he pitched 14 no-hitters. He once struck out 21 batters in a row in a Venezuelan tournament game and 16 batters in a row in a Latin American tournament game. In Willie's own words, "Baseball was my life and the only thing I was really good at. If I didn't make it in baseball, I didn't know what I would do."[3]

Willie's family put immense pressure on him to go to the U.S. and make it big in the major leagues. When he was 16, Willie was signed to a minor league contract by the Texas Rangers. Upon arriving in the U.S. from Venezuela, he was like a fish out of water.

Because he was not able to communicate in English very well and did not have coaches who spoke Spanish, Willie received little feedback on his pitching. He was given the ball and was expected to perform. To make matters worse, Willie didn't have anyone helping him assimilate into the culture of his new country. For the most part, he was left to fend for himself. Homesick and withdrawn, Willie lost his confidence and swagger. He felt threatened, and his Caveman went into overdrive. It's no surprise Willie's performance suffered.

Despite having what scouts unanimously called "major league stuff" (pitching ability), at best, Willie's performance was inconsistent. In his own words, Willie told me, "Whether my performance was good or bad felt like flipping a coin."

Despite Willie's maddening inconsistency, the Rangers continued to believe in his potential. They thought his physical talent might allow him to rise to the occasion and pitch better in the major leagues. The Rangers promoted 19-year-old Willie.

On July 24, 1989, in his major league debut with the Rangers, Willie suffered a meltdown. He failed to record a single out. Facing five batters, he gave up two walks, a single, and two home runs! Mercifully, he was pulled from the game before suffering any further humiliation.

Willie had gone from near prodigy status to a player with only sporadic flashes of talent that were not to be counted on. The game that had been his entire life, the one thing he was truly good at, was slipping away from him. Talk about pressure!

Five days after his disastrous major league debut, the Rangers traded Willie to the Chicago White Sox. A new city, culture, coaches, and teammates awaited him. Willie's confidence was close to rock bottom. However, as in any good movie, the underdog was about to get another chance.

The White Sox assigned Willie to their AA minor league team, the Birmingham Barons. Yes, the same Barons team whose pitching coach was Rick. Willie didn't know it, but his life was about to take a 180-degree turn.

When Rick first started working with Willie, Rick asked lots of questions, listened, and observed. He wanted to get to know Willie before offering any pitching advice. Based on his observations, Rick realized Willie was ill-prepared to be a major leaguer. To put it kindly, Willie's practice habits were not good.

Rick began coaching Willie by establishing a series of skill-building drills. To Willie, the endless repetitions felt like overkill. Willie recalls, "I'd complain to Rick, 'Do we have to do this again?' Up to that point in my career, I had succeeded by relying on my natural ability. I assumed whether I succeeded as a major league pitcher or not depended on my natural ability."

Recall our learning from Chapter 7 regarding the difference between a fixed mindset and a growth mindset. Willie saw his ability as fixed. Rick had a growth mindset, and knew Willie's skills could be developed further.

Every time Willie asked, "Do we have to do this again?" Rick would reply, "Yes, we are going to do it again and again." Rick wanted Willie to understand that, if you aren't able to consistently execute great pitches in the calm of the bullpen where there is no pressure, you cannot expect to do it in the pressure of a game.

Season after season, you go through the same five-day routine to prepare yourself to pitch on game day. Other than game day, being a major leaguer starting pitcher is boring and repetitive. The process we go through to prepare ourselves is not real exciting and not what most people want to hear, but the repetition is your defense against all that's going on around you. Rick constantly preaches, "Trust the process!" It's really what great performance is all about.[4]

—*Jim Abbott, winner of the 1987 James E. Sullivan Award as the nation's best amateur athlete, winning pitcher of the 1988 Olympic gold-medal-winning game versus Cuba, and pitcher of a no-hitter with the New York Yankees*

Rick regularly tells his pitchers, "You need to be able to consistently execute great pitches in any environment, including the toughest environments—whether you happen to be standing on a pitching mound on a cruise ship in the middle of the ocean, or 40,000 feet off the ground, or in Yankee Stadium with more than 50,000 enemy fans yelling at you. To be able to execute great pitches in any environment, you have to be able to do it on autopilot."

In other words, you need to be able to perform at your best under pressure without thinking. A good example of performing a complex skill while on autopilot is driving a car. As an experienced driver, you don't give any thought to what your hands and feet are doing and you make many decisions without conscious thought.

It's worth highlighting that there are big differences between this form of autopilot and the Caveman's reflexive emotional reaction we discussed in Chapter 2. The Caveman's reaction to pressure is a form of unconscious *incompetence*. The autopilot Rick seeks with his pitchers is a form of unconscious *competence*, based on deliberate practice.

The world's foremost authority on acquiring expertise, K. Anders Ericsson, highlights the critical distinction between the version of practice most of us are familiar with and what he refers to as *deliberate practice.*[5] Deliberate practice is characterized by several elements:

- It is designed specifically to improve performance, often with the help of a teacher/coach.

- It can be repeated a lot.

- Feedback on results is continuously available.

- It's highly demanding mentally, regardless of whether the activity is intellectual or physical.

- It often isn't much fun.

The elements of deliberate practice remind me of visiting Rick at the Baltimore Orioles minor league spring training facility. As I arrived, I noticed eight pitching mounds lined up next to each other, with a pitcher on each. A little more than 60 feet away from each mound was a home plate with a catcher behind it. Eight pitchers throwing to eight catchers in the heat of the Florida sun. Nothing out of the ordinary.

Then I noticed something I'd never seen before. Two posts with a string that ran between them, at knee height, across all eight home plates. The eight catchers' gloves were positioned right behind the string. I asked Rick what the string was for. He replied, "193." Seeing me look puzzled, he continued, "That's the major league batting average for balls put in play that were pitched at the height of the batter's knees or lower (author's note for non-baseball fans: .193 is a poor batting average; it's great for the pitcher but not good for the batter).

Rick continued, "The pitchers who learn to hit the string over and over will be successful. The string gives them immediate feedback on whether they've hit their target or not. They practice pounding the string week after week, all spring long. Everyone says they want to be great. Some are willing to pay the price and others aren't."

Part of being a pro is training your mind and your body to the point you don't need to think anymore when you're performing. When you're at that point, you are less susceptible to the debilitating effects of pressure.

The thoughts and actions leading to your best performance are imprinted on your mind.

—*Rick Peterson*

Do You Ever Get Bored?

During one of my conversations with Rick, he shared a story of a conversation he had with Tom Glavine toward the end of his career. Rick was in the clubhouse and was looking through a Press Guide at Glavine's career statistics. At that point, he had played 18 years and had followed the same 5-day routine for each of his roughly 600 starts.

Rick walked into the main part of the clubhouse, where Glavine was alone in a leather recliner, drinking a cup of coffee and watching ESPN. Rick said to Glavine, "Tommy, 18 years! Do you ever get bored of doing the same thing over and over?"

Glavine smirked and responded, "Coach, I never get bored of winning."

> While the process of overpreparing may feel boring,
> the results are spectacular.

Bottom of the 9th, Tie Game

At the Orioles minor league spring training complex, there are four fields. On my first day there, I moved from field to field to see what the players were working on. I stopped at one field to watch what looked like an intra-squad game.

I noticed a runner on 3rd base. The pitcher stared at the sign from his catcher and delivered the pitch. The batter smoked a line drive into the outfield and the runner on 3rd base scored easily. At the conclusion of this play, I heard a loud voice from an older man in uniform, standing behind the pitcher's mound. Presumably, he was the manager or one of the coaches. He yelled, "We need a better pitch than that. Let's do it again. Bottom of the 9th, tie game, one out, runner on 3rd." For those who aren't well-versed in baseball, this is a high-pressure situation; its execution determines the winner and loser of a game.

The runner who had scored on the previous play ran back out to 3rd base, a new batter came to the plate, and play resumed. This time, the batter hit a ground ball, the fielder looked at the runner on 3rd base to hold him there, and then he threw the ball across the diamond for an out. The runner remained on at 3rd base. My mind instinctively shifted to the fact there were now two outs, a slightly less precarious situation. To my surprise, the coach behind the pitcher's mound yelled, "That's better. We need a strikeout or a ground ball. Let's do it again. Bottom of the 9th, tie game, one out, runner on 3rd."

The team repeated this same high-pressure situation over and over and over, at least a dozen times. Because they were repeatedly exposed to the threatening situation, the players developed their skill, their confidence, and their comfort level with the challenging situation.

When the situation you've practiced over and over presents itself in a game—when the outcome really matters—you're filled with confidence because you know you've performed well in this same situation countless times.

Your mind is your master and your body is your servant. Your body is never going to outperform your mind. The only way you can keep your mind calm is when you're prepared for anything.

—*Rick Peterson*

When you are repeatedly exposed to a perceived threat, you will find that the situation is no longer threatening.

When performing, you will not only be ready for the pressure situation, you will look forward to it!

Not Seeing Is Believing

During my conversation with Wilson Alvarez at the Orioles minor league spring training facility, he shared the lesson that turned around his career.

> After I'd started learning what it means to prepare like a professional, Rick changed things up on me during one of our bullpen sessions. He asked me to throw a pitch with my eyes closed. I had no idea why, but I went along with it. After I made the pitch and heard the ball pop in the catcher's glove, Rick said, "Okay, open your eyes. Was that a good pitch or a bad pitch?" I said I thought it was a good pitch. He confirmed it was. We repeated this again and again and again.

Soon Willie was consistently hitting the catcher's glove with his eyes closed. "I was amazed I could *feel* and hear myself making great pitch after great pitch without seeing my target. Then Rick asked me a question I'll never forget: 'If you can consistently execute great pitches with your eyes closed, why don't you believe you can do it in a game, when you have your eyes open?'"

These "eyes closed" bullpen sessions helped Willie believe for the first time that he would succeed in the major leagues. By preparing harder than what would be expected of him in any game performance, the 100-pound weight of game pressure soon felt like a feather. Willie stopped pressing. He started to relax and performed with soaring confidence.

In 1991, at age 21, almost two years after his disastrous first major league start, Willie made his *second* major league start. He threw a *no-hitter!* In doing so, he became the first player in major league history to fail to record an out in his first game and throw a no-hitter in his second game. Willie played 13 seasons in the Major Leagues, earning almost $31 million. He is now in his mid-40s and works with rookie pitchers in the Orioles minor league system. "Everything I have, I owe to Rick. I want to give these kids what he gave me. He taught me how to be a pro. He believed in me. He taught me how to believe in myself."

Familiar with Chaos

The world's greatest swimmer is Michael Phelps. He is the most decorated Olympian of all time, with a total of 22 medals from the 2004, 2008, and 2012 Olympics. Eighteen of those 22 medals are gold, twice as many as the next Olympian.

Not only is Phelps legendary for his medal count, within the swimming community, he's equally legendary for his training. For about five years, he did not take one day off. That includes training on Christmas Day and his birthdays. Phelps's coach, Bob Bowman, shares one of the key techniques he used to prepare Phelps to perform his best under pressure. Bowman calls it making the world's greatest swimmer "familiar with chaos."[6]

Bowman created uncertainties for Phelps in lower-risk situations so he was ready for anything when it mattered most. Before meets, Bowman hid goggles so Phelps had to swim without them. Because of Phelps's extreme preparation, he already knew the number of strokes it took to reach from beginning to end; thus, he could swim the race blindly.

Another time, Bowman intentionally stepped on Phelps's goggles to create cracks. When submerged, chlorine water filled Phelps's goggles, stung his eyes and caused blurriness. This almost maniacal level of preparation proved incredibly valuable during the 200-meter butterfly in the 2008 Beijing Olympics.

When Phelps dove into the pool to start that race, his goggles malfunctioned. After the race, Phelps told reporters, "My goggles started filling up more and more. At about 75 meters left in the race, I could see nothing. I couldn't see the black line. I couldn't see the T. I couldn't see anything. I was purely going by stroke count. And I couldn't take my goggles off because they were underneath two swim caps."[7]

Far from being rattled, Phelps continued swimming blindly. He was confident he could do it; he had done it before many times. The result? When Phelps looked up at the clock, he had not only won the gold medal, but he had also broken his own world record!

One thing that makes it possible to be an optimist is if you have a contingency plan for when all hell breaks loose. There are a lot of things I don't worry about, because I have a plan in place if they do.

—*Randy Pausch,* The Last Lecture

When you prepare for *harder-than-you'll-ever-need* conditions—for chaos—you develop the skill and confidence to handle anything.

Highlights

- Heed the lesson Rick learned from MJ: talent does not equal performance; preparation equals performance. It's the difference between unleashing your full potential or not.

- The boost you get from overpreparing is often more mental than physical. You tame your Caveman, your confidence soars, you relax, and your brain releases performance-enhancing chemicals.

- Overprepare to the point where you are unconsciously competent—performing at your best without thinking.

- Repetition during normal conditions is good, but not enough. Like Willie throwing his bullpen sessions with his eyes closed, practice in conditions that are tougher than you'll ever face in competition. Then, during the competition, you can Try Easy.

- Like Michael Phelps, prepare for the worst and get familiar with chaos. Breed confidence and relaxation by knowing you're ready for anything.

Try This

- As you prepare for your next high-pressure performance, define what overpreparing looks like. Answer the question: *What does tougher-than-I'll-ever-need preparation look like in my situation?*

- Now do it. Go through the process of overpreparing. Answer the question: *Am I able and ready to perform on good autopilot, without thinking?*

- After overpreparing, assess whether you are more confident and relaxed.

Final Thoughts

Man does not simply exist but always decides what
his existence will be, what he will become the next
moment. By the same token, every human being has
the freedom to change at any instant.[1]

—*VIKTOR FRANKL*

Every day and in every moment, you can choose what to think.
Your choice on what to think impacts how you feel, what
actions you take, and the results you reap. Tomorrow morning,
will you choose to wake up to an alarm clock? Or are you better
served to reframe the start of your day and wake up to an opportunity clock?[2]

At crunch time, will you choose to listen to the reflexive, primal,
performance-crippling emotions of your Caveman? Or will you
choose to pause and challenge your Caveman, consciously reframing to see and act upon the opportunity?

When you see the world through the lens of opportunity, life is
so much better. You think better, feel better, and produce better
results. You are your best when it matters most.

The battle for your mind is fought daily. Be encouraged as you
have the knowledge and motivation you need to win the battle.
Rick and I have shared numerous examples of how others move
from threat to opportunity on command, enabling them to come
through at crunch time. Take a moment to jot down your favorite

stories, the ones you want to remember and begin applying to your pressure situations. Appendix A provides the index of stories.

Genius is the ability to put into effect what is in your mind. There's no other definition of it.

—*F. Scott Fitzgerald*

Reframing is a muscle of the mind. Give it a workout and the muscle becomes stronger. The stronger the muscle, the easier it becomes for you to look past threats and see opportunities. The "Try This" section at the end of each chapter (and combined in Appendix B) gives you specific guidance on how to get started. Whether your pressure situations occur at work, in sports, in school, or at home, the reframes we've shared are universal.

As you build your reframing muscles, share your knowledge, your excitement, and your results with others. Coach your loved ones, your teammates, your classmates, and your colleagues. Not only will it help them, it will help you.

It's critical to have support. You have to have people around you that at least share enough of your ethos to be part of that ensemble. People that also remain calm and understand that being in a place of no fear is how you figure things out and perform best.[3]

—*Steven Soderbergh*

Help make reframing pressure from threat to opportunity contagious!

Please share your feedback on the book, your questions, and your success stories with us via email at *judd@juddhoekstra.com* or at *facebook.com/CrunchTimePerformance*.

A

Index of Stories

B

Try This

The "Try This" sections that appear at the end of each chapter are combined here to guide you through getting started with reframing during crunch time.

Chapter 1: Reframing—The Shortest Path from Threat to Opportunity

- Identify a high-pressure situation you're facing now or will be facing in the near future (e.g., completing a big project with an impending deadline, making an important presentation to a challenging audience, performing in a game or a recital, taking a final exam). Use this situation as the context for practicing the skill of reframing as you read this book.

- Write down what you're currently thinking and feeling about your high-pressure situation.

- Are you seeing it as a threat or an opportunity? If a threat, come up with two ways to think about it as an opportunity.

- If you can already see the opportunity, write that down.

Chapter 2: Why Reframing at Crunch Time Is Necessary

- Using the high-pressure situation you identified in Chapter 1, walk through and capture notes regarding the first two steps of the reframing process.
    - Pause and recognize your Caveman's story. *Do I want to think or feel this way?*
    - Challenge your Caveman's story. *Is this fact, fiction, or the opinion of others?*

Chapter 3: Reframing from Trying Harder to Trying Easier

- Identify one specific activity where trying your hardest may be hurting your performance.
- Develop a game plan for how you can throttle back to a relaxed 90-percent effort.
- Put your game plan into practice and compare the results of your performance with the two methods.
- Adjust your effort as needed to reach optimal performance.

Chapter 4: Reframing from Tension to Laughter

- Think about what amuses you, makes you smile, or makes you laugh. It could be anyone or anything.

- For your sources of humor that are recorded or available online, gather these into an easily accessible place (e.g., your smart phone).

- Tap into your sources of humor the next time you're getting ready for a big performance. Reap the performance-enhancing benefits of your laughter.

Chapter 5: Reframing from Anxiety to Taking Control

- Identify a daunting, outcome-oriented goal that has you feeling under pressure.

- Figure out your version of "Hit the glove!" by chunking it down into one or more simple, short-term, bite-sized, process goals. If you're still feeling intimidated, chunk it down further until you've got it to a point where the process goal seems relatively easy.

- Recognize and reward yourself for the progress you make on this process goal. Your confidence will grow and your brain will thank you with a dose of dopamine. This will help you keep your momentum.

- If you aren't already, begin practicing mindfulness—meditation, prayer, journaling, or physical exercise such as walking or yoga—to calm your mind and enable you to see pressure situations with a fresh perspective.

Chapter 6: Reframing from Doubt to Confidence

- Identify a pressure situation where you have doubts you will come through at crunch time. Try one or more of the following to boost your confidence:

  - Remember you don't need to feel great to perform great.

  - Recall your hours of preparation. If it helps, total up the number of hours you've prepared for this situation.

  - Travel to a time and place in the past when you performed very well and picture yourself there in the present.

  - Make two lists: one list of your strengths that will help you perform well in this situation, and another list with the actions you will take to overcome your fear, worry, and doubt.

Chapter 7: Reframing from Failure to a Learning Moment

- Reflect on how you typically respond to undesirable outcomes. Consider whether this response is hurting or helping future performance.

- Ask yourself:

  - *What am I learning from these situations? How can I change my mindset now?*

  - *How does this inform how I'll prepare for similar situations in the future? How will I seize an opportunity from a disaster?*

  - *Does my new game plan give me confidence that I will perform better at my next opportunity?*

Chapter 8: Reframing from Prepared to Overprepared

- As you prepare for your next high-pressure performance, define what overpreparing looks like. Answer the question: *What does tougher-than-I'll-ever-need preparation look like in my situation?*

- Now do it. Go through the process of overpreparing. Answer the question: *Am I able and ready to perform on good autopilot, without thinking?*

- After overpreparing, assess whether you are more confident and relaxed.

Acknowledgments

There are so many people who have contributed to this book, many directly and many indirectly. Because my career spans over 30 years, countless people have influenced my life and shaped my perspective.

To my dad, Pete Peterson, I feel very privileged to have grown up in a baseball family and on a baseball field. My dad gave me a Pittsburgh Pirates uniform to wear when I was two years old and I haven't taken a uniform off since! His excellent leadership qualities as a player, scout, manager, and general manager for the Pirates and New York Yankees deeply influenced my understanding of the game and how it is played. His loving guidance helped shape my life.

I'm forever grateful to my mother for teaching me integrity, fairness, compassion, and generosity. Thank you to my three sons, Sean, Derek, and Dylan, who are my three jewels. Thank you to my sister, Amy, for being a great friend.

When I chose the path of being a coach and teacher, it was clear to me that to be a master teacher, I needed to be a master student. I'm humbled and grateful to all the people along the path of my journey who have been my teachers. The common thread for all of us is to truly make a difference in the quality of people's lives.

I'm grateful to all the pitchers I've coached, with special thanks to those who contributed to this book: Tommy Glavine, Chad Bradford, Jim Abbott, Barry Zito, Wilson Alvarez, and Jason Isringhausen.

To all the teams I've been part of, I'm honored to put on their uniform and be part of this great sport of Major League Baseball. In particular, many thanks to Willie Randolph, Jim Duquette, Ken Macha, Art Howe, Billy Beane, Dan Duquette, and Buck Showalter. To all my current colleagues at the Baltimore Orioles, it's a privilege to work with you.

Many thanks to all my friends and thought leaders who contributed to this book: Mark Levy, Bill Squadron, Billy Beane, Dr. James Andrews, Chris Correnti, Willie Randolph, John Feinstein, Brett Machtig, Art Howe, Joe Favorito, Laurie Cameron, Steven Soderbergh, Susan Torroella, Ilyssa Levins, and my colleagues at Wharton Moneyball Sirius XM—Matt Johnson, Dr. Adi Wyner, Dr. Massey Cade, Dr. Shane Jensen, and Eric Bradlow.

Deepest gratitude to T.Y.S. Lama Gangchen Rinpoche, a source of constant inspiration and guidance. Without him, this book would not have been written.

—*Rick Peterson*

'm incredibly grateful for the opportunity to get to know Rick. Dos Equis has it wrong; *Rick* is the most interesting man in the world. I thank him for welcoming me onto his team with open arms, for the wisdom he shared throughout our journey, for his humility, and for his friendship. We share a passion for helping others be their best.

A huge shout-out to Mark Levy, *the* positioning expert for thought leaders. He helped us identify the big idea for this book and craft a winning book proposal. Rick and I are deeply grateful for his curiosity, creativity, humor, and friendship.

Thank you to our publishing team at Berrett-Koehler. Rick and I chose to team with them because they gave us a voice every step of the way. Special thanks to Neal, Steve, and Jeevan for serving as our Sherpas.

I'm in awe of Ken Blanchard for his abundance mentality. He's shared many opportunities with me, including this one.

In addition to the expert contributors Rick mentions earlier, thanks to the following individuals for their expertise and friendship: Dr. Julie Bell, Madeleine Blanchard, Jim Conroy, Mac Delaney, Ed Hiner, Tom Kelly, Kate Larsen, Linda Miller, Garry Ridge, Andrew Tarvin, and Lisa Zigarmi.

I appreciate the family members, friends, customers, and colleagues who read the draft manuscript and provided me with invaluable feedback and encouragement: Ron, Claudia, Jeff, and Josh Hoekstra; Sean Storin; Kelly Burling; Brian Soczka; Ryan Beacom; Jamie Blattstein; Carla DiGiovanni; Suzanne Sherry; Brian Hennessy; Randy Lott; Don Sandel; Chris Edmonds; Nicole Pappas; and Martha Lawrence.

Last on the list and first in my heart, I'm eternally grateful for Sherry, Julia, and Cole. Their sacrifices during this three-year journey are too many to count. I'm thankful for their continuous encouragement and for their desire to reframe pressure alongside me. They inspire me daily to tame my Caveman and be my best for them.

—Judd Hoekstra

About the Authors

RICK PETERSON is known throughout professional baseball as a leading practitioner for peak performance coaching. He has a cutting edge approach to coaching and maximizing performance by combining biomechanics, predictive analysis, and methods to master the mental game. His track record has been chronicled in Michael Lewis' bestseller *Moneyball* and John Feinstein's *Living in the Black*.

During his 15 years as a Major League pitching coach with the Oakland A's (during the Moneyball years), the New York Mets, and the Milwaukee Brewers, he has coached Hall of Famers, All Stars, and Cy Young Award Winners including Hall of Fame pitchers, Tommy Glavine, Pedro Martínez, Trevor Hoffman, as well as Barry Zito, Mark Mulder, Al Leiter, Tim Hudson, Jim Abbott, Billy Wagner, Johnny Franco, and many others. He has also worked with many other elite athletes like Roger Clemens and Michael Jordan.

Rick is currently the Director of Pitching Development for the Baltimore Orioles. As a sought-after motivational and inspirational speaker, he frequently appears on national radio and television shows—ESPN, Bloomberg TV, MLB (Major League Baseball) Network, Fox Business, Wharton Moneyball on Sirius XM—to share his expertise.

Always innovative and cutting edge in his approach, Rick is a pioneer in saber metrics and biomechanical analysis to keep pitchers healthy and reduce injury. He was awarded the Dr. Andrews Lifetime Achievement Award from the Academy of Sports Medicine Institute, the Cal Ripkin, Sr. Player Development Award from the Baltimore Orioles, and Charlie Lubin Coach of the Year Award with the Chicago White Sox.

What is well-known among his players, but was a secret until *Crunch Time*, is Rick's expertise with the mental side of the game. He is a master coach in helping others reframe situations to achieve greater success and maximize their potential.

Rick believes that giving back is a critical ingredient to success; he volunteers with numerous charities and is a United Nations NGO Representative and Peace Ambassador with a global humanitarian foundation.

He has three sons and lives at the beach in New Jersey with his wife, Lelia.

Rick is a sought-after keynote speaker who enjoys speaking with audiences of all sizes. He shares his expertise and reframes people's thinking through a wealth of engaging stories and coaching methods. He speaks on coaching, peak performance, leadership, innovation, performing under pressure, leadership lessons from Moneyball, reframing, and predictive analytics. Rick can be reached at *rick@rickpetersoncoaching.com* or *www.rickpetersoncoaching.com*.

JUDD HOEKSTRA is a leadership and human performance expert, sales executive, bestselling author and speaker. Along with Dr. Ken Blanchard, Judd is a coauthor of the bestselling *Leading at a Higher Level* as well as *Who Killed Change?* He is also the coauthor of a number of leadership programs and performance-enhancing tools offered by The

Ken Blanchard Companies. Judd received Blanchard's prestigious Founders' Award faster than anyone in the 37-year history of the company. The award recognizes Judd for his outstanding contribution to Blanchard's intellectual property.

In his Vice President, Central Region role, Judd serves on a sales leadership team responsible for developing sales strategies with accountability for top-line revenue growth, bottom-line profitability, and the enhancement of Blanchard's purpose-driven, high-performance culture. Judd is also responsible for coaching a regional team of leadership solutions advisors to achieve individual and regional revenue and profitability targets.

Judd also serves targeted customers as a leadership solutions advisor. In this role, Judd leads high-performing teams for some of Blanchard's strongest client partnerships.

Judd received his bachelor's in business management and marketing from Cornell University, where he played hockey and baseball. He also graduated from the Advanced Business Management Program at Kellogg Graduate School of Management. Judd and his wife, Sherry, live in the Chicago area and are the proud parents of Julia and Cole.

Judd enjoys speaking and consulting with teams and organizations in a variety of industries. His areas of expertise include performing under pressure, leadership, coaching, reframing, and change. The clients he teams with describe him as focused on both results and people, as well as collaborative, innovative, humble, and fun. Judd can be reached via email at *judd@juddhoekstra.com* or on the web at *facebook.com/CrunchTimePerformance* or at *juddhoekstra.com*.

Endnotes

Introduction: Rick and Izzy

1. Baseball-Reference.com, box score for Oakland A's vs. New York Yankees on October 11, 2001, *www.baseball-reference.com/boxes/NYA/NYA200110110.shtml.*

Chapter 1: Reframing—The Shortest Path from Threat to Opportunity

1. Kate Larsen, interview by author, telephone, March 10, 2014.

2. Andrew Razeghi, *Hope: How Triumphant Leaders Create the Future* (San Francisco: Jossey-Bass, 2006).

Chapter 2: Why Reframing at Crunch Time Is Necessary

1. Steven Soderbergh, interview by author, telephone, April 17, 2014.

2. Ryan Whitwam, "Simulating 1 Second of Human Brain Activity Takes 82,944 Processors," *Extreme Tech*, August 5, 2013, *www.extremetech.com/extreme/163051-simulating-1-second-of-human-brain-activity-takes-82944 processors.*

3. Paul D. MacLean, *The Triune Brain in Evolution* (New York: Springer, 1990).

4. Daniel Goleman, *Emotional Intelligence* (New York: Bantam Dell, 2006).

5. Dr. Steve Peters, *The Chimp Paradox* (New York: Penguin Group, 2013).

6. Evian Gordon, "Getting Away from Pyramid Selling," Squire to the Giants, November 15, 2015, *https://squiretothegiants .wordpress.com/tag/evian-gordon/*.

7. David Rock, "What Inequality Does to Your Brain," *Huffington Post*, November 10, 2011, updated January 10, 2012, *www .huffingtonpost.com/david-rock/psychology-of-inequality_b_ 1075227.html*.

8. Scott G. Halford, *Activate Your Brain* (Austin, TX: Greenleaf Book Group Press, 2015).

9. Dr. Steve Peters, *The Chimp Paradox* (New York: Penguin Group, 2013).

10. Garry Ridge, interview by author, telephone, May 13, 2014.

11. Madeleine Blanchard, interview by author, telephone, May 6, 2014.

Chapter 3: Reframing from Trying Harder to Trying Easier

1. Try Easy is a concept and phrase used frequently by peak performance author, speaker, and consultant, Dr. Robert Kriegel, author of *Performance Under Pressure* (Lake Mary, FL: Archer Ellison Publishing, 2010).

2. Tom Verducci, "The Left Arm of God," *Sports Illustrated*, July 12, 1999.

3. Sandy Koufax with Ed Linn, *Koufax* (New York: Viking Adult, 1966).

4. Steven Soderbergh, interview by author, telephone, April 17, 2014.

5. Mark Levy, interview by author, telephone, November 10, 2015.

6. Wikipedia, "Steve Cohen (magician)," *https://en.wikipedia .org/wiki/Steve_Cohen_(magician)*.

Chapter 4: Reframing from Tension to Laughter

1. Andrew Tarvin, interview by author, telephone, December 28, 2015.

2. Randy Garner, "Humor, Analogy, and Metaphor: H.A.M. It Up in Teaching," *Radical Pedagogy* (2005).

3. Thomas Ford of Western Carolina University cited by Eric Jaffe, "Awfully Funny: The Psychological Connection between Humor and Tragedy," *Association for Psychological Science Observer* (May–June 2013), *www.psychologicalscience.org/ index.php/publications/observer/2013/may-june-13/awfully-funny.html*.

4. Constantine von Hoffman, "Uses and Abuses of Humor in the Office," *Harvard Management Communication Letter* (February 1999).

5. Alice M. Isen, "Positive Affect Facilitates Creative Problem Solving," *Journal of Personality and Social Psychology* 52, no. 6 (1987).

6. Mayo Clinic Staff, "Stress Relief from Laughter? It's No Joke," (n.d.), *www.mayoclinic.org/healthy-lifestyle/ stress-management/in-depth/stress-relief/art-20044456*.

7. Amy Toffelmire, "Ha! Laughing Is Good for You!" Canoe. com (April 2009). *http://chealth.canoe.com/channel_section_ details.asp?text_id=4982&channel_id=11&relation_id=27881*.

8. David Abramis, "All Work and No Play Isn't Even Good for Work," *Psychology Today* 23, no. 3(1989).

9. Thomas E. Ford, Brianna L. Ford, Christie F. Boxer, and Jacob Armstrong, "Effect of Humor on State Anxiety and Math Performance," *Humor: International Journal of Humor Research* 25, no. 1 (2012).

10. Christopher Robert, "The Case for Developing New Research on Humor and Culture in Organizations," *Research in Personnel and Human Resource Management* 26 (2007).

11. C. W. Metcalf and Roma Felible, *Lighten Up: Survival Skills for People Under Pressure* (New York: Basic Books, 1993).

12. R. Cronin, *Humor in the Workplace* (Rosemont, IL: Hodge-Cronin and Associates, 1997).

13. Mac Delaney, interview by author, Naperville, IL, December 30, 2015.

14. Jim Abbott and Tim Brown, *Imperfect* (New York: Ballantine Books, 2012).

Chapter 5: Reframing from Anxiety to Taking Control

1. Chad Bradford, interview by author, telephone, February 3, 2014.

2. Dr. Hendrie Weisinger and J. P. Pawliw-Fry, *Performing Under Pressure* (New York: Crown Business, 2015).

3. Dr. Julie Bell, interview by author, telephone, April 2, 2014.

4. Dr. Julie Bell, *Performance Intelligence* (New York: McGraw-Hill Education, 2009).

5. Bill George, "Developing Mindful Leaders for the C-Suite," *Harvard Business Review*, March 10, 2014.

6. Ibid.

7. Liz Neporent, ABC News, "Seattle Seahawks Will Have 'Ohm' Team Advantage," January 30, 2014, *http://abcnews .go.com/Health/seattle-seahawks-ohm-team-advantage/ story?id=21614481.*

Chapter 6: Reframing from Doubt to Confidence

1. Billy Beane, interview by author, telephone, February 13, 2014.

2. Chad Bradford, interview by author, telephone, February 3, 2014.

3. Tom Glavine, interview by author, telephone, February 7, 2014.

4. Barry Zito, interview by author, telephone, February 4, 2014.

5. Mariano Rivera, *The Closer* (New York: Little, Brown and Company, 2014).

6. Dr. Julie Bell, interview by author, telephone, April 2, 2014.

Chapter 7: Reframing from Failure to a Learning Moment™

1. The Learning Moment is a trademark of the Learning Moment Inc.

2. Garry Ridge, interview by author, telephone, May 13, 2014.

3. Tony Robbins, *Unlimited Power* (New York: Free Press, 2008).

4. Tom Glavine, interview by author, telephone, February 7, 2014.

5. John Feinstein, interview by author, telephone, February 24, 2014.

6. John Feinstein, *Living on the Black* (New York: Little, Brown and Company, 2008).

7. Ibid.

8. Ibid.

9. MLB.com, Video, MLB Network, "Glavine Inducted into HOF," July 27, 2014, *http://m.mlb.com/video/topic/6003532/v34856591/glavine-is-inducted-into-the-baseball-hall-of-fame.*

10. Carol Dweck, *Mindset: The New Psychology of Success* (New York: Ballantine Books, 2008).

11. Lisa Zigarmi, interview by author, telephone, June 5, 2014.

12. Martin Seligman, *Learned Optimism* (New York: Vintage Books, 2006).

Chapter 8: Reframing from Prepared to Overprepared

1. Tom Glavine, interview by author, telephone, February 7, 2014.

2. Jim Conroy, interview by author, telephone, October 8, 2015.

3. Wilson Alvarez, interview by author, Sarasota, FL, March 20, 2014.

4. Jim Abbott, interview by author, telephone, February 10, 2014.

5. K. Anders Ericsson, Neil Charness, Robert R. Hoffman, and Paul J. Feltovich, *The Cambridge Handbook of Expertise and Expert Performance* (New York: Cambridge University Press, 2006).

6. Frederick E. Allen, "You Can Only Win in Sports, or Anywhere Else, if You're Ready for Chaos," *Forbes*, August 14, 2012, *www.forbes.com/sites/frederickallen/2012/08/14/you-can-only-win-in-sports-or-anywhere-else-if-youre-ready-for-chaos/#1aaf2d763f6f690016823f6f*.

7. Unnamed CBS News Correspondent, "Michael Phelps on Making Olympic History," CBS News, November 25, 2008, *www.cbsnews.com/news/michael-phelps-on-making-olympic-history/*.

Final Thoughts

1. Viktor Frankl, *Man's Search for Meaning* (New York: Touchstone, 1984).

2. Motivational speaker Zig Ziglar regularly insisted he woke up each day to an opportunity clock.

3. Steven Soderbergh, interview by author, telephone, April 17, 2014.

Index

R

radio analogy, 7–8

Rangers, 94, 126

reflexive reaction and thought, 20, 85. *See also* threats

reframing. *See also* mindfulness; mindsets

    applying, 27

    availability of, 11

    Cakebread Cellars example, 9

    challenges as opportunities, 9–10

    Cole's hockey tryout, 28–30

    definition, 7

    efficiency of, 11

    examples of, 5–8

    explained, 16

    flexibility of, 11

    goals of, 8

    importance of, 4

    Korean War example, 9

    as muscle of the mind, 140

    practicing, 35

    Reagan's reelection example, 9–10

    speed of, 11

    steps to, 30–33

    teaching, 11–12

    threats as opportunities, 33

    Tribe's Thinking, 101–105

    value of, 10–11

repetition. *See* practicing

reptilian complex. *See* Caveman

results and actions, changing, 4–5

Rick and Izzy. *See* Isringhausen, Jason "Izzy"; Peterson, Rick

Ridge, Garry, 31, 101–105, 118

Rivera, Mariano, 93–95, 98

Robbins, Tony, 105

Rock, David, 25–26

Roosevelt, Theodore, 76

S

sales organizations, working in, 74–75

Schueler, Ron, 72–73

SEALs, confidence of, 86

seasons, chunking, 90–91

seeing is believing. *See* not seeing is believing

self, comparing with self, 76

self-doubt, moving beyond, 89, 98

self-evaluation, choosing method of, 79, 83

self-talk

    of Caveman, 22–23

    of Conscious Thinker, 24–25

    example of, 7–8

Seligman, Martin, 112–113, 117

setbacks, dealing with, 116

setup man, Mo as, 93–94

Sharpies, breaking out, 58–60

Sherry, Norm, 44

situations, handling, 12–13

skill-building drills, engagement in, 127

skills, 10,000-hour rule for mastery, 11

Smith, Dean, 123

Soderbergh, Steven

    on calmness, 45–47

    on panic, 19

    on support, 140

Berrett–Koehler
Publishers

Berrett-Koehler is an independent publisher dedicated to an ambitious mission: *connecting people and ideas to create a world that works for all.*

We believe that to truly create a better world, action is needed at all levels—individual, organizational, and societal. At the individual level, our publications help people align their lives with their values and with their aspirations for a better world. At the organizational level, our publications promote progressive leadership and management practices, socially responsible approaches to business, and humane and effective organizations. At the societal level, our publications advance social and economic justice, shared prosperity, sustainability, and new solutions to national and global issues.

A major theme of our publications is "Opening Up New Space." Berrett-Koehler titles challenge conventional thinking, introduce new ideas, and foster positive change. Their common quest is changing the underlying beliefs, mindsets, institutions, and structures that keep generating the same cycles of problems, no matter who our leaders are or what improvement programs we adopt.

We strive to practice what we preach—to operate our publishing company in line with the ideas in our books. At the core of our approach is stewardship, which we define as a deep sense of responsibility to administer the company for the benefit of all of our "stakeholder" groups: authors, customers, employees, investors, service providers, and the communities and environment around us.

We are grateful to the thousands of readers, authors, and other friends of the company who consider themselves to be part of the "BK Community." We hope that you, too, will join us in our mission.

A BK Business Book

This book is part of our BK Business series. BK Business titles pioneer new and progressive leadership and management practices in all types of public, private, and nonprofit organizations. They promote socially responsible approaches to business, innovative organizational change methods, and more humane and effective organizations.

Berrett–Koehler
Publishers

Connecting people and ideas
to create a world that works for all

Dear Reader,

Thank you for picking up this book and joining our worldwide community of Berrett-Koehler readers. We share ideas that bring positive change into people's lives, organizations, and society.

To welcome you, we'd like to offer you a free e-book. You can pick from among twelve of our bestselling books by entering the promotional code **BKP92E** here: http://www.bkconnection.com/welcome.

When you claim your free e-book, we'll also send you a copy of our e-news-letter, the *BK Communiqué*. Although you're free to unsubscribe, there are many benefits to sticking around. In every issue of our newsletter you'll find

- A free e-book
- Tips from famous authors
- Discounts on spotlight titles
- Hilarious insider publishing news
- A chance to win a prize for answering a riddle

Best of all, our readers tell us, "Your newsletter is the only one I actually read." So claim your gift today, and please stay in touch!

Sincerely,

Charlotte Ashlock
Steward of the BK Website

Questions? Comments? Contact me at bkcommunity@bkpub.com.

Certified

Corporation
bcorporation.net